A Memoir: On Love and Life
Frederick E. Curtis II

Copyright © 2015 Frederick E. Curtis II
All rights reserved.

ISBN: 0986128406
ISBN 13: 978 - 0986128400

For Granny and CeAndra

Contents

Preface: So, What Is This?

1	Life: The Sharpest Pain
2	Love: Glory and Restoration: Don't Waste Your Possibilities
3	Love and Life: The Way the Wind Blows
4	Life: The Affectionate Pain
5	Love: Don't Waste Your Heartache
6	Life: Pain and Porn
7	Life: INsecurity
8	Love: Help
9	Love: For What the System *Can* Be
10	Love: For the Game
11	Love: For God

Preface: So, What Is This?

"A life without love is a life without purpose, so when I say I love you, I really mean it."

I wrote that quote some years ago. I guess you can say it's somewhat of a motto for me. That's how I wanted to live my life. That's how I still want to live my life. Some days are easier than others when it comes to living out that altruism.

If you are reading this, odds are you know me or know of me, you have seen or met me, or maybe you have worked with me—we've likely crossed paths with one another at some point in this lifetime. If none of these cases apply to you, then this book is so much bigger than I ever intended it to get, and so many people whom I never realistically dreamed of reaching are actually reading my words. That could be because of a number of things, a list of which I'll spare you, but whatever the reason, I'm happy you picked it up.

One of the most precious things we human beings get is time. I know it can be hard to reconcile that concept. On one hand, time in so many ways is useless and decrepit. It's a man-made concept that takes something as infinite and awe inspiring as the universe and constructs it into a manageable measurement that our fallible and minuscule minds can comprehend. In the grand scheme of things, you can't measure time—not because you're not smart enough or need to learn the theory of relativity or buy a new clock, but because in reality, time just doesn't exist. As I write this, it's 12:52 p.m. on the Eastern Seaboard of the United States. But how do we *know* it's 12:52? Who determines that it's 12:52? How many institutions have to continue to be protected and to flourish for it being 12:52 (now 12:53) to matter anyway?

In the grand scheme of things, time doesn't really exist, because it doesn't really matter. Now that we've got that out of the way, thanks for taking the time to pick up this book, because as arbitrary as our attempt at measuring time is, it is truly valuable. Even though we, as humans, can't adequately ascertain it, time is one of the most important things we terrestrial beings get. It is more valuable than gold and more sacred and embracing than intimacy, and it determines our destinations and legacies far after we return to the ground. Time is, in fact, of the essence.

I make a lot of juxtapositions. (You'll get used to it.) Some of them, I have clear understandings of; others I write about simply in an attempt to understand. There are a lot of things I do not know, and I acknowledge that for 89.7 percent of the things I do not comprehend about life right now, I still won't comprehend them when my life is over. I'm OK with that.

So, as I said, I'm happy you picked up this book. I'm happy you took the time to read it…this far anyway. You may find it exhilarating. You may find it funny. You may find it boring. Each of us has our own way of interpretation. I decided to write about my life for a number of reasons, the two most important of which are love and life. Funny, huh?

Love and life has been my parting shot, my calling card, and my conclusion, if you will, for a number of years. I put it at the end of blogs and letters, and by the time you read this, it may or may not be tattooed somewhere on me. So what does it mean?

I love hard. Some people say that saying is simply an excuse for being overly sensitive and emotional, while others say it's another way of saying I'm a stalker who expects you to love with a deep, unconditional affection in return. You'll quickly learn that at this stage of life, there are a handful of people's opinions that I actually care about, at least when it comes to me and how I feel.

What else about me? I have a lot of feelings, and I'm really good about communicating them. I use to be ignorant, self-conscious, and insecure, believing that only women were permitted to share their feelings and emotions at the rate that I do. I've grown up a lot since then. I've been though my fair share of struggles and triumphs, but I have come to recognize that all of those things are simply designed by the creator of the universe to bring glory and praise to the creator of the universe. That's a big part of why I chose to write this. It would be so unbelievably selfish of me to only share everything that I've learned as a result of my afflictions with the people closest to me.

A Memoir: On Love and Life

My pain drives me. It motivates me. It makes me who I am. When it's two o'clock in the morning and I've got a big exam or a huge assignment or project due and my eyes get weary and the bed or couch starts calling my name, I tap deep within my soul, clutch the deepest and darkest grips of the stuff I've seen and been through, and proceed to finish the task at hand. That's just me. But I woke up one day and realized that as I get older, grow in my relationship with Christ, and begin to see the world with different lenses and through a different perspective, that pain is slowly dissipating. In other words, Christ is actually healing my wounded and broken heart. (Weird, huh?)

As I recognized this, I came to the conclusion that I had to share this pain with others. I have to share my heartache and brokenness with other people who may be going through similar or worse circumstances than I am. To not share this pain would be arrogant, selfish, and impious of me (among so many other things).

So I've spent a lot of time talking about time and pain when I should be telling you what love and life mean to me. I did that on purpose. Time and pain are both immeasurable. We can't touch time, and we can't touch pain—not the pain I'm talking about, anyway. In some sort of weird, abstract way, we know that both time and pain exist in some aspects, and they mean a lot for the time being, but as time progresses, so too does the depth of your pain. My pain comes from the people and things in this life that I love and have loved the most. I firmly believe that, as they say, it is better to have loved and lost than never to have loved at all, because after you love and then lose it, you at least have a story to tell, lessons to teach others, and mistakes to grow from. Curiosity might have killed the cat, but since we're all going to die at some point anyway, we might as well make the most of the experience.

  Love is life. It's what makes us who we are. Love is at the very core of each and every one of us. We all love some things. We all love some people. We are living. If I did not have the things I love the most, my life would be totally pointless, purposeless, and not worth living. That same concept and idea likely applies to you. Time used to be the most important thing in the world to me. Pain was how I motivated myself and how I endured some of the most grueling and challenging phases of my life. I used to be defined by time and pain. Then I met Christ. When I met Christ, I realized that my life was nothing more than a vapor—I'd be here today and gone the next. I realized that time, that man-made measure of something that's actually immeasurable, is in God's hands. I realized that the Spirit truly does comfort. God really does love me. Jesus really does heal the wounds. So, once I met Christ, I could no longer define myself by time and pain—it just wasn't possible to do so anymore.

That's where love and life come in.

Love is who I am. Love is at the very core of what is me. Love is my life. I long to consume my life with love: love for God, love for people, and love for sharing the love and message of God with His people. Love for the Gospel. Love for helping to make the lives of people better. Love for giving people hope—in this life and, most importantly, in the next. Love for seeing people in love. Love for letting people know that they are loved—for making them feel loved and for sharing the greatest love story known to man. That's what I love. That's my life. I want you to experience this same devotion, this same kind of affection, commitment, and unconditional nurturing. I've found it. It wasn't easy.

As you read through these pages, you'll learn that I am not the same person I used to be. God took me through so many valleys before He allowed me to experience this joy, and I fully expect that more trials are yet to come. Even so, I find peace in knowing that, from this point forward, whatever life may bring, I will endure it with love.

I've found the greatest love of all, and a huge part of that is, in fact, loving yourself, but I find love for myself through Christ, through the scriptures, and through devoting my life to loving others. That's what love is to me. That's what life is to me. Time and pain are both temporal. Love and life, at least the life I am focused on, last forever. Now, let's talk about life.

A Memoir: On Love and Life

Chapter 1
Life: **The Sharpest Pain**

It was around midnight, perhaps a little before or after. I don't remember the date, the month, or even the year. As I think back on it, those details are useless anyway. This was one of those memories that you don't need an arbitrary date or season to identify with. Pain has that sort of effect on a person. On one hand, some of the deepest, most painful moments of your life are most identifiable with the brisk chill of the autumn wind or the smell of the flowers as winter washes away. This wasn't one of those times.

We'll just say it was midnight. I had been asleep for a while. Moms made dinner early. (I call my mother "Moms," by the way.) I ate. I suppose it had been a long school day, or whatever she made was just so good that it put me right to sleep. Either way, I knocked out cold pretty early. I woke up around eleven o'clock, lying on the bottom bunk of the bed that I shared with my little brother, Russ. My parents were still together at the time; I could hear bits of their conversation every now and then.

It was a peaceful night. That is, I remember it as peaceful because I don't remember it as being filled with fear, although that may simply be a product of having endured too many fearful nights.

I don't remember how old I was. I would venture to say I was either eleven or twelve, in the sixth or seventh grade. It was a school night. I remember that part vividly. I tossed and turned repeatedly. There was a wall to the left of the bunk bed. Puberty had just started to hit for me, which meant—well, a lot of things. My wall was covered with pictures of women, from Serena Williams to Nicole Ari Parker. No one made a big deal of this. I think it's just what you expect from a soon-to-be-teenage boy. Those images lined the wall adjacent to my bed. The right side of my bed was open to the room, but I had taken a sheet from the linen closet and folded it into the railing of the top bunk, providing me with a small amount of privacy. I wanted a place I could go and at least feel like I was alone, even though I felt that way so often to begin with.

At the end of the bed, I had a semiorganized stack of magazines and papers. I've always been a writer. I had notebooks and tablets filled with lyrics and poems. Every sports preview magazine known to man was in that stack too. I'd read them occasionally. That stack was where I went when I was angry, which was quite often. When I got mad, angry, or confused, I wrote. My writing was quite different then, as you could probably imagine. It was littered with cursing and other obscenities, but that was the best way I knew to express myself at the time. In so many ways, that stack of notebooks and magazines, along with *The Blueprint* and *The Marshall Mathers LP*, helped me navigate my emotions through a fairly rough childhood.

That bottom bunk was my domain. It was my space. It was my area. It was where I went when I wanted to be alone or when I wanted to write. When I wanted to feel or be or do or imagine something that no one would feel or be or do or imagine with me, that's where I went. However, those moments were always so incredibly short-lived.

Those pictures to the left helped my mind concoct images they had no business creating. Those notebooks helped me write out my frustrations to a certain degree. Those sports magazines helped me dream about living an impossible dream. That bottom bunk did so much for me, and yet it couldn't begin to address the issue that caused me the most unquenchable and consequential pain.

Everything I did to that bottom bunk was an attempt to cover up how I felt about the top. The top was where my heart was. The top was the source of so much of my frustration, angst, and anxiety—so much of my love, and yet so much of my anger. For a time, the top was the reason I even ventured to believe that there was no God, or at the very least that God couldn't be nearly as good, loving, or just as everyone tried to make Him out to be. The top bunk was where so many questions about life and its meaning and purpose began to develop.

Russ slept at the top. He liked it up there better. When we were younger, we had shared a bed—twin sized, if I recall correctly—but Russ and I were getting way too big to share, so my parents went out and somehow got what every pair of little brothers wants: a bunk bed.

But wait—get those images of that stainless steel, modern Sears bunk bed out of your mind. This wasn't it, but I'm glad it wasn't. Our bed was made of a nice, dark wood. Please don't ask me to describe what kind of tree it came from, because I couldn't begin to tell you. I vaguely remember putting it together, and I *do* remember it took my dad and me nearly an entire day to make it happen. That day came and went, and the impact of that bed lived on far past its dismantling.

Russ, who was eleven years old, five years younger than me, wasn't too big when we got the bunk beds. At first, he took the bottom and I took the top, primarily because my folks were a little worried he would fall from the top. (The truth is, that eventually happened anyway. Don't worry about Russ, though—by the time it happened, he was older. He was always a trouper, my little brother.) Funnily enough, after a couple of weeks, he made his way down to the bottom bunk on a nightly basis, and we ended up sharing one single-sized bed instead of a twin. As he got older and bigger, we kept that tradition alive, except instead of resting on the bottom bunk together, we switched to the top. I always made sure his body was closer to the wall. My legs would serve as a shield to keep him from falling off the right side of the bed, and every night before I got into bed, about an hour or two after Russ, I would add a layer of pillows and blankets at the foot of the bed, where a fall could potentially occur, just to make sure all bases were covered.

You can say Russ, and that top bunk, were my world in more ways than one. So that night, around eleven, I woke up. I sat in my bed, looking straight up at the wooden panels that kept the mattress from falling and suffocating me. As I studied the texture and swirls of the panels, I couldn't think of anything besides the life that lay breathing there on the top.

I think it was around this time when I first began to recognize that there was something different about Russ. I didn't know what that difference was. I didn't know what that difference meant for me or for Russ or for my family, but I knew *something* was different. At eleven years old, different is not good. Different is not comforting. New is good. New makes you feel warm and fuzzy. New helps you fit in with the cool kids who have five different colors of the exact same kind of sneaker. New would have been just fine, but Russ, well, he was certainly no longer new. He was different.

I had noticed this before. I can't pinpoint a time or place or explanation as to when I discovered that something was different about him, but I like to think I was a somewhat smart kid. Russ and I, separated only by five and a half years, never had a typical brotherly relationship, at least not the kind you would expect from brothers so close in age.

That's not necessarily a bad thing. I loved Russ. I love Russ. I will always love Russ. But as I got older and realized that Russ was different, I didn't know how to manage that or who to blame for it. I was so amazingly frustrated by what I thought shouldn't be happening or taking place. In my mind, Russ shouldn't be different, and he and I should be enjoying the kind of relationship every pair of brothers has. God had different plans.

I got out of bed. I suppose it was around 11:15 p.m. by this time. I paced the room. It was dark. Before I got into bed every night, I would usually turn the light in the bathroom on so as to slightly lighten the hallway right outside our bedroom. At the time, I would say I was doing it mostly for Russ, but in reality, I left that light on 70 percent for myself and 30 percent for Russ.

I had gone to bed very early that night, so the bathroom light was not on. The lamp in my parents' bedroom on the desk by my mother's side of the bed was on. It was dim, but it was enough to partially light up my room in the process. The hallway was black. We had curtains on the window. That limited the amount of illumination from the street lights outside. There I was in the dark. Pacing. I did that for about ten minutes. I suppose it was about 11:25 p.m. I sat down on the bottom bunk once more. I was thinking. I was dreaming.

I was thinking about all of the things Russ and I couldn't do. I was dreaming about all of the things Russ and I *should* be able to do. I thought about what our futures would be like. I thought about what kind of life he would have. I wondered if, when he started going to school, the kids would be as mean, cruel, nasty, and dismissive as they were to me. I dreamed about him being healed. I dreamed about him waking up the next morning, reading an entire children's book from front to back, and telling me everything about his day like he was a young protégé on his way to Stanford to study architectural engineering.

I stopped thinking and dreaming at about 11:40 p.m. I stood up. The room was still dark. My mother's lamp was still on. The door to my sisters' room to the right was closed. It was just me, and I was just standing there. I had on an old Allen Iverson T-shirt. That shirt was so old that the picture of A. I. was from his rookie year, before he had cornrows. I stood there in my T-shirt and basketball shorts. For the next twenty minutes or so, I stared at Russ. He was sleeping. He still had a little baby fat, especially in his face. He had a pretty sharp haircut too.

When it came to sleeping, Russ was like my sisters. Normally, he slept with the covers over his head. Not tonight. The covers were a little below his chest. His face was turned toward the window, facing me. He had his right arm slightly below his cheek, as if the cushion of the pillow wasn't enough. A hint of saliva partially dripped from his lip, but not enough to saturate the pillow cover.

I stood there. I looked into his eyes, even though his eyes were closed. I graced my hand across his shoulder and then over his hair. I just looked at him. I talked to him for a little bit. I don't recall what I said. I reckon I made him a ton of promises that night, some I've been able to keep, others I am still working on, and some I'll never be able to make happen. That's partly why I don't make promises. Making promises is stupid. It's useless. As much as I may want to do something to you or for you, I have very little control over anything. I can't make you a promise, simply because there's a much higher probability of me breaking it than coming through on it. That night taught me not to make promises, along with so many other things.

I don't know what it was. I couldn't describe what triggered it or what made it come about. The conversation I had with Russ that night took my emotions to a place I don't think they had ever gone in the first twelve years of my life. After I talked to him and made him a ton of promises I would eventually break or fail to come through on, I kissed him on the cheek. I think that's what did it.

Moments later, I started sobbing. You could even say I started wailing. I wasn't crying. Crying is what you do during the climax of a great romantic movie. You cry as a child when you get shots or stitches. I cried when Barack Obama won the presidential election in 2008. That moment, after I spent twenty minutes in the silent dark talking to Russ and kissed him on the cheek, that moment showed me the difference between crying and sobbing.

After about two or three minutes, my parents heard. My mother came in first and asked me what was wrong. I didn't want to wake Russ up, so I took her by the hand as she gently picked me up from the edge of the bed. By this time, my hands and shirt were littered with tears and snot. You could have reasonably thought I had just jumped out of the shower with my clothes on.

My dad noticed I had been sobbing and asked the same question, "What's wrong?"

I didn't know how to answer this. It's the age-old question. I've been asked "What's wrong?" so many times in my life, but this is the one that sticks out the most. If I knew what was wrong, if I could really communicate what was hurting me and what was causing tears to balloon out of my eyes like rain from the sky in Central Florida every summer midday, I probably wouldn't be here. To a certain degree, however, I knew what was wrong. I knew what was causing me so much grief and heartache and anger. I knew what I wanted to say, but I just didn't know how to say it.

Sometimes, it felt like Russ's difference was something that the family constantly swept under the rug. In retrospect, I know that wasn't the case. In fact, sweeping it under the rug was probably the exact opposite of what happened—for everyone except me. It was a topic of conversation, of course, between my parents, and even more so with my two older sisters. That aggravated me. To some degree, it still does. I understand why everyone thought keeping me out the loop and playing the naïveté card was the best thing for me. I suppose they wanted to protect me (whatever that means). Maybe they didn't want me to know that Russ was *really* different, or that Russ potentially had some things that were permanently different about him. I get all of that. Years later, I feel like those things may have caused more harm than good, but there's grace for us all in every single circumstance.

"Tell us what's wrong," my mother whispered as she rubbed my back

"What's wrong, Fred?" said my father. (Don't worry; that tone doesn't adequately communicate just how sensitive and caring he was in this moment. Just know that he was.)

A few more seconds went by. I managed to reasonably compose myself. I used the neckline of my T-shirt to wipe away some of the excess snot below my left nostril, using my hands to redirect the flow of the tears from my cheeks, sucking and snorting in the residue that I couldn't quite reach with my shirt. And although I had no idea how to say it or even what to say, after a few more seconds of sobbing and wiping away tears, I answered the question. "I just wish Russ could communicate like the rest of us can."

What followed felt like the most silent three seconds of my entire life. I don't know what my parents' initial reaction to my statement was. Instantly, after uttering the word *can*, I was back to square one. It was almost like I hadn't spent the last twenty-five minutes crying. My tear ducts worked overtime that night. A fresh new shipment of tears and snot began to flow.

I assume my parents probably looked at one another. I have no idea what they said—they didn't say anything out loud but communicated with each other nonverbally. Both of them knew it. Once you have kids and you've been married for a certain amount of time, it doesn't really matter how good or bad the relationship is, you've got an uncanny ability to communicate without saying a single word. I'm sure at that moment they had the same response.

After those three seconds, my mother offered the best and most reassuring words any mother could, "I know. Me too, baby boy, me too."

My dad followed suit. I don't quite remember what he said, but I'm sure it was comforting, at least temporarily. I don't remember much else about that night. I don't remember when I stopped crying. I don't remember getting back in the bed. I can't tell you what T-shirt I changed into after I finally got myself together (though I am 100 percent sure I had to change).

So much of that night, after the thinking and dreaming and sobbing, is a monumental blur. I think my life changed that night. Those tears connected me to myself in ways that had never happened before. Finally, for a split second, I realized how I felt about something important to me, and though that was a feeling filled with pain, frustration, and despair, it was the beginning of my life in one way—and the beginning of my love in another.

I've always loved Russ, but I haven't always showed it. My heart hasn't always been as big as it is, and taking care of and looking after him hasn't always been my greatest motivation in life. I was selfish, mean, and intolerant for a large portion of my childhood. Heck, there are still times when I'm selfish, mean, and intolerant, but never on the scale that I was then. I thought the world revolved around me—and if it didn't, then it definitely *should.* I thought I should always get my way and get what I wanted. I felt like I had the right to do and say as I pleased at any moment. I need look no further than my own wicked heart to see practical application of the fact that no man is righteous and we are all born into sin.

Anger. Guilt. Frustration.

I don't remember much before the age of six. I think that's one of the complexities of life. It's one of those things I think I want to ask God about once we get to heaven, at which point I will likely sit for a moment and come to the realization that nothing about this earth will matter once we get there. The memories of my early childhood are fleeting. I know the gist of the scientific explanation for this: the part of our brain responsible for memory is not fully developed until a certain age, so we don't explicitly remember things from our early childhood.

I get it.

But I would love to ask God why that is. Why can't we remember the simple days of being an eleven-month-old, when the biggest care we had in the world was when someone was going to recognize that we needed a new diaper? Why don't we recall the hundreds of dollars Mommy and Daddy spent on our birthday party at the age of two? Would it have been so tough for you, God, to help us remember a little of what it was like to be the crown jewel at our first Thanksgiving, being passed from hand to hand and having to endure everyone's sweet potato pie breath?

These aren't accusations against God. After all, no man can bring a charge against the self-existing one. They're just simple questions I ponder when I have a little too much time on my hands. But there's a connection.

A Memoir: On Love and Life

I was five and a half years old when my brother was born. I cannot with any certainty recall anything that happened in my life before January 7, 1997, but I remember asking my parents for one thing that I longed for and cherished and wanted the most: a little brother.

I've never asked my parents about this. I'm 92 percent sure they didn't choose to have another child, embarking on the journey, the trials, the expenses (among other things) that come along with welcoming another human life into the world solely based on a five-year-old's desire to have a playmate. Even so, that statement is at the cusp of much of the anger, guilt, and frustration I felt relating to my little brother during the first years of his disability.

I'm an absolute sucker for babies, especially the fat ones. If you're fat and you're a baby, you can absolutely get anything out of me that you want, which I assume will include holding you as long as physically and humanly possible.

I remember that Russ was a fat baby. That's about all I remember. I don't have much recollection of his first few years on earth, except that he was loved, he was adventurous, and he took after me, his older brother. That phenomenon started early. Whatever I indulged in, Russ loved indulging in it as well. We were always like two peas in a pod. I've got two older sisters. The oldest, Yasmin, isn't necessarily a spring chicken. My other sister, Ashleigh, is three years older than me. Yasmin and I often talk politics and other complexities of the world. Ashleigh, who I simply refer to as Lee, was my partner in crime. I *love* all of my siblings, but Russ and I were Michael Jordan and Scottie Pippen circa 1992: back-to-back world championships, Olympic gold medal on the dream team…global icons. No one could dream of touching us, let alone sniffing our gym shorts.

I qualify that time so vividly because life changed so rapidly. Russ got older. I got older. My siblings got older. My parents got older. It seemed, as everyone got older, that everyone also grew more distant and further apart. My parents had their issues, as they always did, but it never hindered the relationship between Russ and me. We were always bystanders to their problems, but it never affected the way we interacted with one another like it did my sisters. But then, in the words of Taylor Swift, everything started to change.

Age brought about recognition, accompanied by a heavy dose of uncertainty and a teaspoon of fear. Russ was about three years old...he may have just turned three. I was coming down the hallway, probably intent on raiding the kitchen for a frosted strawberry Pop-Tart and whatever sugary drink they advertised on cartoon network at the time. My parents were sitting in the kitchen at the round table in the corner. I suppose this was one of those times when they weren't separated, or weren't openly having issues. As I was about to cut the sharp right, walk onto the kitchen tile and open up the refrigerator door, I heard them talking. Moms said, "I think we should go get Russ evaluated."

At once, my heart suddenly stopped and my stomach dropped as if I was on a rollercoaster at Six Flags. In retrospect, it was easy to see from some of the ways he interacted as a toddler that Russ might have had *some* condition. Perhaps he was dyslexic. Maybe Russ was just going to be a slower learner than everyone else in the family. Maybe he would talk with a lisp or just develop a tad slower than other kids his age. That was always the dream scenario, at least in my mind. Everyone had kept me away from the reality for so long that it was going to be hard for me to accept the truth.

At that age, I didn't know what *evaluation* meant, but I knew it wasn't an ideal word. I'd started noticing Russ's communication difficulties when he was almost three, and because I was an eight-year-old kid who noticed that he didn't quite talk as much or make as many sounds as other soon-to-be three-year-olds, I know my sisters and parents recognized this fact long before I did.

Needless to say, Russ didn't stay three years old, and I didn't stay eight. And my parents didn't stay together. And for a brief moment in my life, I blamed Russ for that. Hindsight is twenty-twenty. You can judge me all you want for being twelve years old and blaming my seven-year-old brother for the problems in my parents' marriage, but at that age, I didn't know any better. I was angry. I was bitter. I was frustrated with the world. No one would listen to me, and certainly no one cared to feel or hear how Russ's disability was affecting me. (At least that's how I felt anyway.)

I was angry. At first, I was angry with Russ. It seemed like everyone loved Russ more than they loved me—that every waking minute of the day was spent tending to Russ, thinking about Russ, or researching what might help make Russ better. I felt like the black sheep, the one everyone cast away to the side and told to go play outside until the streetlights came on. My anger caused me to resent Russ, only for a brief period of time, but a period of resentment nonetheless.

I hated being around him. I hated going anywhere with him. I hated sharing a room with him. I hated that Russ always wanted to sleep under me and be near me. I hated that whenever I wore my baseball cap to the back, he just *had* to do the same. It irked me that because I was drinking fruit punch, he *had* to drink fruit punch. It got under my skin that when I jumped off the stairs and skipped the last step, he jumped off the stairs and skipped the last step. These things were so utterly annoying not because Russ looked up to me or wanted to be like me, but because I felt the relationship was so one sided.

When I'd told my parents I wanted a little brother, I had never imagined he would be anything like Russ. All I had seen was friends and family members with younger siblings or children. I thought about how much fun it would be to have someone to play video games with. I dreamed of how awesome it would feel to have another person run my imaginary Kids Basketball Association draft every November. (I can still reel off all the teams in that league by the way. Fascinating stuff indeed.)

    I thought about playing basketball in the front yard for hours on end. I thought about staying up late talking about who was the best of the Power Rangers (I was always a black ranger kind of guy, by the way) while making a list of the girls we liked. I figured Russ and I would be like all of the examples of brothers I'd seen on television. We would do absolutely *everything* together and nothing would ever separate us. Russ would understand me in a way that no one else on earth would ever understand me.

    This is what I longed for, dreamed for, and hoped for.

    I needed it more than anyone will ever truly know. Even at five and a half, I felt alone a lot. I look back at all of those moments and experiences and recognize that it was for the greater good. I know now that God was simply preparing me for a lifetime of leadership, servitude, and sacrifice. As Margaret Thatcher once put it, you can't lead from the crowd[1], and I have learned that lesson more than once throughout life. I embrace that. I relish that. I cherish that. I am now able to prepare for my moments of solitude or melancholy during the seasons of joy and abundance. But as a child, I had no ability to do these things.

I *needed* Russ to be everything I imagined he would be. Sure, it would be a while before these things could happen—after all, my brother would be an infant and toddler for a few years—but I figured I could put up with that. I'd felt this wave of emptiness for so long, I could feel it for a few more years, at which point Russ would help me release it.

My parents' issues tie into this complexity. My dad was in and out of the house—not so much in and out of my life, but certainly the house. I felt the strain of that. Even when things seemed to be going right for them, there was a perceived disconnect between my father and me—he never seemed to be interested in what I was interested in. Pops rarely wanted to play video games. He rarely wanted to watch sports. He seldom sat

---

[1] Margaret Thatcher, *The Downing Street Years*.

and watched a cartoon. In retrospect, I don't blame him. I played a lot of video games and watched a lot of sports, and now that I've worked for a few years, I know how demanding and draining it is to support a family financially. (So do not take this as an assertion that my father was not there for me or that he never delighted in the joy of spending time with his children, because he did; he still does.)

With that said, I think that was precisely one of the primary reasons why I wanted a little brother so much. I didn't expect my dad to want to play video games and watch *Dexter's Laboratory* all night. That was what I needed Russ for.

I knew no one would understand or let me vent when Moms or Pops upset me about something trivial. That's what Russ would be there for.

I knew people would simply tell me that words can't hurt me and that God made me the way I am for a reason, but Russ would be there to comfort and then punch me in a weird, perplexing way that only a brother can.

I didn't need my dad to do all of the things he probably just didn't have the time or energy to do, because I knew, once

Moms told me she was pregnant, that Russ would fill in all those gaps for him.

As you have no doubt guessed, this didn't turn out as I had planned.

I was angry with Russ, but that anger didn't stay directed at him for long. I was smarter than that, even at such a young age. I knew he didn't ask to be born. I knew he didn't ask to have his disability. I knew that, if he could, he would probably change things around too.

It took me a while, but I realized, even at the age of twelve, that Russ wanted all the things I wanted so much more than I did. In reality, I think it pained him more than it did me that those dreams didn't come to fruition the way I'd planned. I know all he ever wanted to do was see me smile, make me happy, brighten my day, be my joy, play basketball, and eat Pop-Tarts with me.

A part of me is still nauseous that I ever felt resentment toward him.

You live and you learn, I suppose.

The next two or three years were filled with guilt. In other words, I took responsibility for Russ's predicament.

In my mind, I felt that if I hadn't told my parents I wanted a little brother, Russ wouldn't have been born, and he would be better off not having experienced earth than dealing with the frustrations of his disability.

In my mind, because I had asked for Russ, my parents' marriage had dissolved. To me, it didn't matter that they'd had their troubles before, or that Russ was probably nowhere near the top few reasons they divorced. None of that mattered. In my mind, if I hadn't been stupid enough to ask for a little brother, Russ's disability wouldn't have caused a strain on their relationship, and my parents would have found some way to stay together.

I felt that maybe it was something I did wrong as a child: maybe it was the Gummy Bears I stole from the drugstore one night; or it was the girl's butt that I grabbed while running down the hallway; or it was the late Showtime movies that I snuck downstairs and watched after midnight. (Grace, my friends.

Grace.) Regardless of what it was, I felt that my own shortcomings had caused Russ's autism.

I know. You are probably thinking there's no possible way this could be my fault. To an adult mind, that's an easy assumption to make. But when I was thirteen, it was crystal clear to me that Russ's inability to communicate like most other eight-year-olds was my fault.

I had done something. I didn't know what it was. I didn't know how to rectify the situation. I didn't know what, if anything, I could change to make things remotely better.

I was hopeless. I was shameful.

Russ would never fully live the life I or his parents or his siblings imagined he would, and that ate me alive at such a young age.

I hated myself for it.

At that point, my guilt began to blend with anger. I wasn't angry with Russ anymore. I had learned better than that. I was angry at the world.

I was angry with every classmate who did everything with his or her sibling. I was angry with teachers who had kids who participated freely in every after-school activity. I was infuriated with every "short bus" joke that was uttered.

I felt guilty, but I was mad too. I hated school. I hated the world. I hated God. I was sad. I was empty. I was lonely.

The guilt, along with my anger, subsided over time. I matured a little, which means I learned how to properly channel all those negative emotions. Even so, I wish I could say I stopped blaming myself. I wish I could say I learned to see the silver lining in the situation. I wish I could say that Russ miraculously got better, my parents found a way to solve their issues, and both of my sisters ended up going to college close to home.

I wish I could say these things. But as you very well know, life is not a fairytale. Innocent people die. Bad guys get off. Beautiful, faithful women and men are cheated on. People who long for and chase after and desire God more than anything else…well, they go through suffering.

Throughout high school, that last part fit me best. What had been anger for one year and guilt for four more slowly transformed into frustration. I educated myself more on autism. I started seeing my parents' situation for what it truly was and realized there was nothing I could have done to salvage it. I began recognizing some of the complexities of life that only come with age.

At this juncture, I came to an important realization: there was nothing *I* could do to change Russ's condition. I could do everything in the world under my power to help make his life better; to make him smile; to make him happy; to help give him all the resources that could help make him the best Russ he could be. I could do all of those things. But I came face-to-face with the startling truth that I was not God—I did not have a magic wand with magical tricks and magical potions that could fix the universe. In essence, I finally came to grips with the fact that I wasn't Harry or Hermione. (This hurt me deeply.)

I can do everything for everyone else. I've always kind of had that ability, so when I realized this (along with my parents' situation) was one thing I could not change no matter what I did, I felt helpless.

That helplessness led to emptiness.

That emptiness led to loneliness.

That loneliness led to frustration.

That frustration almost led me to contemplate suicide.

I look back on those moments and wonder if I *really* had the guts to kill myself or if I was just so desperately crying out for attention and some psychiatric help. I genuinely believe it was both.

I remember one time fairly vividly. Moms and I had had an argument. I can't remember what it was about. It was obviously trivial and irrelevant. I stormed up the steps, but not in a way that would result in her demanding I come back down the steps. I didn't want to draw any attention to myself. I drifted up the steps and walked directly into the kitchen.

I remember the knife I picked up. It wasn't the sharpest tool in the drawer, but I figured it would do the trick. It had a yellow handle. Moms used it to cut up chicken breasts when she made stir-fry or chicken tacos.

I took the knife into the bathroom and locked the door. I got on my knees to pray. Who was I praying to? I couldn't tell you. I didn't have much of a relationship with God at the time, but I reckon I believed in *something*.

I don't think I ever went an extended period of time thinking there was *nothing* else out there, if only because I contemplated killing myself too much to believe that this was the end. In my mind, something else had to be out there, because this place was so overwhelmingly dreadful. Even if I slipped into an eternal nothingness, I had made the determination a number of times in my head that some form of nothingness would be exponentially better than an ongoing cycle of a broken heart brought on by bearing witness to a failed marriage and a disability with no cure.

I hated life. I wanted it to end. It seemed like the best decision.

After all, as a teenager, you don't quite grip the finality of death. I think you're able to understand that you die, and your mind can fathom the fact that you won't be around for the next summer vacation or the NBA finals, but wrapping the mind around the eternality of death—I think that's tough for most kids.

I didn't realize that Ashleigh had seen me go into the bathroom. She must have alerted my mother. Thirty seconds later, my mother came storming up the steps. She seemed angry. She ran an in-home daycare at the time, and it was early evening—there were still two or three kids waiting to be picked up by their parents. She was probably just ready for them to go. It was past the agreed-upon 6:00 p.m. pickup time, and maybe she had plans for the evening; or maybe she just wanted to go take a hot bath. Maybe she was as psychologically drained from everything going on her life (Russ, the marriage, her children, finances) as I was.

I don't know. To be honest, I don't really care to know.

I could hear her footsteps as she made her way from the carpeted stairs to the hardwood floor. She came to the door of the bathroom and beat on it profusely. She wasn't even using her hand—it was the handle of one of the plastic kitchen utensils she used to discipline my sisters and me.

I actually preferred this punishment method to the belt. It had a nickname, in fact; my siblings and I called it "the spoon." It was plastic. It didn't hurt too much. It concentrated all of the force into one specific area, so though the sting was a bit more severe, it didn't last nearly as long as a belt would. So while being spanked was never a pleasure, at least it was the best possible version of it.

She banged on the door some more. There I was, still on my knees. The knife was sitting to the left of me, on top of the toilet seat. I can still feel the softness of the bathroom rug on the floor. I think it was at that moment I realized: I don't *really* want to do this…at least not like this.

That's probably one of the reasons the United States has such an absurd homicide rate, because an absurd amount of people have firearms. There's an emotional aspect of firing a gun, don't get me wrong, but it doesn't take a rocket scientist to know that you can get someone to fire a gun at another individual far faster than you can get someone to stab a person or slit his or her throat. The knife requires relative proximity. I have to be near you. I feel your body heat. I feel *you*. I'm much more likely to experience and draw upon your fear and uncertainty. All of these emotions are present with a gun, but they aren't as consuming; they don't move you in the same way.

So when it came to trying to take my own life with a knife, I just didn't have the guts. I didn't want to die *that* badly. I wanted it to end, but I didn't want to be the one to stab myself repeatedly and then die an awful, slow, agonizing death. That would be no fun. I figured halfway through the occasion, as I lay on the bathroom floor bleeding profusely while holding my stomach and naturally applying pressure because one of my natural bodily and humanistic instincts would be to try and stay alive, I would start to question my decision, and somewhere in my physique, I would think to myself, "Maybe the grass isn't greener on the other side."

I never thought I'd get to the other side, but I assumed that would be me. That's why I reckon people who hang themselves kick their legs much longer than people who are sentenced to die by hanging. If you're sentenced, you don't have much stake in the matter. The choice has been made for you. Whatever time you have left after your sentencing, whether it is mere seconds or weeks or decades, you're much more likely to emotionally and psychologically come to grips with it. You've prepared your mind for that moment when the rope engraves itself around your neck. There's no need to kick. This is the end. It comes as no surprise. I presume that's what it's like anyway. I only write from the perspective of a kid who was suicidal for a considerable amount of his childhood.

I came to grips with my reality. Like I said, I didn't want to do this…not this way anyway. It would be too painful. It wouldn't be quick enough. My sister would never be able to walk into a bathroom without feeling discomfort again. My mother would feel guilty. All of those reasons sound good, and they did play some role in my decision, but the main reason, 90 percent of the reason I didn't follow through on any of my suicidal temptations was—you guessed it—Russ.

Russ didn't deserve that. Russ needed me. After all, *I* already felt alone. *I* felt like no one cared about my feelings. *I* felt like the black sheep. In the midst of those emotions, I could only imagine how Russ felt.

If I felt alone, I knew his loneliness was multiplied to the tenth degree. If I felt like no one cared about my feelings, I know he felt like everyone around him was a brick wall when it came to empathizing. If I felt like the black sheep, he must have had times when he felt like the adopted stepchild.

I can't qualify all of these things with him. But I'm pretty sure these are feelings that were there. It would have been unbelievably selfish of me to take my own life and disappear into oblivion, while leaving him here to live with the pain of it all afterward. That's not what a good brother does.

So, after about six seconds of listening to Moms knocking, I opened the door. It was kind of funny actually. I waited those six seconds for a reason. The first second or two of knocking was brief. It lacked sympathy. It lacked emotion. Those two seconds of knocks were cold. They were absent any compassion. In those knocks, I felt a sense of mockery, almost like, "I know you're not *really* about to take your own life, so open up the (insert expletive) door."

That felt disrespectful and completely dismissive to me. I was used to feeling dismissed, but not on that level. This was a complete disregard for who I was, where I was as a teenager, and how I was feeling about life. I couldn't stand for that. So I stayed there, positioned on my knees, for a few more seconds.

Don't count too fast in your head. This isn't some hide-and-seek game. Think about the slowest six seconds of your life, and this is it. Like time ticking down at the end of a Super Bowl.

That third second came. I looked around the bathroom. I knew I was going to open the door; it was just a matter of when. I looked up. I saw the mirror to my right and the clear shower curtain with the gold emblems. I took in the lavender paint and the flowery wallpaper. I think for a moment I legitimately considered becoming an interior designer.

Seconds three through six may have honestly changed my life. The first two seconds made me as angry as I have ever been. They validated my claims—not that no one cared about my well-being or whether I had enough to eat or whether I woke up the next morning, but that no one genuinely cared just how worthless I felt inside.

Things quickly changed.

If those first two seconds were the most emotionless seconds of my life, the last four compensated for them. It was almost like I could feel the legitimacy in those last four seconds. She knocked harder, this time with more fervency and a sense of urgency. By second number four, it felt like, for an instant, she had given my feelings the respect they deserved; finally, if only for a brief moment, someone felt the same pain, emptiness, and uncertainty that I did.

A Memoir: On Love and Life

That was all I ever wanted. That was all I ever needed. (Spoken in my Backstreet Boys voice…don't worry if you're too young to understand that reference. Google it.) At that point, during my period of deep and solemn frustration, what meant the most to me wasn't changing my circumstances. I understood that no one could change Russ. I had finally become content with that. For me, I just simply wanted someone to at least act like I mattered. I wanted a chance to sit with or talk to or be held by or be with someone who acted like they understood how I was feeling, even if they really didn't. It didn't matter to me if they were putting on a performance that would rival that of Heath Ledger in *The Dark Knight*. For a moment, if only for a brief moment, it would have meant so much to me to be someone's focal point; for someone to tell me they understood what I was going through and how I was feeling; to tell me that every little thing would be all right. I wouldn't have believed them, but that would've been enough to get me through the moment. It would have been enough to get me through the day, until the next suicidal thought came tangoing into my brain.

I finally opened the door. My feelings had been given the respect they deserved. My threats, at least for two seconds, had been recognized. I was content. It didn't matter what happened after I opened that door, those two seconds, and thinking about Russ, were enough to face whatever challenge came my way.

You could imagine what took place next. Unbeknownst to me, my mother teed off, wailing me with lethal strikes from the spoon. (If you're a law enforcement agency or anyone who is even remotely thinking about claiming this was child abuse, stop it. Please. Thank you.)

They were all on the arms. I was a fairly athletic kid, so they didn't really hurt. I think I shed a few tears, if only because spankings don't begin to stop until you cry a little. It was over in a matter of seconds…six seconds, I suppose.

Those twelve seconds were, arguably, the most profound twelve seconds of my life. A knife and a spoon revealed unto me things I had been searching to find for years before. My mother's reaction is far from what most suicidal teenagers would expect. If you grab a knife and run into the bathroom with it, you expect, upon opening the door, a hug, a kiss, or a question—some level of compassion.

What did I get?

I got a spanking.

And in that moment, in those twelve seconds, I wasn't angry with my mother. I didn't resent her. I didn't hate her. I didn't want to cause any harm to her. Afterward, I didn't want to cause any harm to myself (for a while, anyway).

Those twelve seconds taught me, and continue to teach me, just how frustrated Russ feels all the time.

I saw taking my own life as a way out. In life, no one understood me. They couldn't grasp the depth of my pain or the hollowness of my sorrow. No one knew what it was like to have your folks separated or fighting all the time; to come to grips with a permanent disability in the person you care most about; to be picked on relentlessly at school and have no one defend you; to be left at home with your father who you're scared of while your mother and sister go out on mommy-daughter dates and don't come back for five or six hours.

No one understood the amount of tears I cried at night. No one could fathom how I felt. Finally, after those twelve seconds, I knew, as best I probably ever would, how Russ felt every day.

I finally understood his frustration and realized mine was incomparable. From that day forward, I vowed to be everything to him that no one else, up to that point, had ever been to me.

Above all things, I am, and will always be, my brother's keeper.

Chapter 2
Love: Glory and Restoration: Don't Waste Your Disabilities

God is funny. He works in his own strange and peculiar ways. He has a sense of humor too—a good one. This I know.

The month was October. The year was 2008. I was a wide-eyed freshman at the University of West Georgia in Carrollton, Georgia.

It wasn't particularly chilly that night. In fact, I think the weather was about as perfect for October as you could ask. One of the Bible study groups on campus was having an event, and I had decided to attend. I lived on campus, and the venue was about a ten-minute walk away from my ten-by-twelve dorm room, so I figured I would go to the event, hear some words about Jesus, grab a late-night meal from Chick-Fil-A, and come back and play *Madden*.

It's funny how this moment even came about.

I had gone to the computer lab a few weeks earlier to print something off. Since I didn't have a printer of my own and wasn't particularly fond of spending money (both facts remain true to this day), I went to the only place I knew of that had free printing.

I had a Bible on me. Don't ask me why I had it. Don't inquire about what I was reading. Don't ask where it came from. In retrospect, I fully acknowledge that it was one of those providential moments in my life—an event brought about and designed by God that eventually helped changed my worthless life up to that point and transform it into something that could bring Him glory. (Yes, Calvinist, that paragraph was just for you.)

I sat down at the computer and printed what I needed. My memory sucks. I don't remember what I was printing. It was later in the afternoon. It was late September, and that means it was football season, so there were plenty of statistics and previews and game reviews to read on the Internet.

It was Georgia, so it still felt like the end of July. There was not a cloud in the sky. Usually the computer lab was full and there was a line that extended far outside the entrance. That wasn't the case right now. Everyone had gone home or back to their dorm rooms to get ready for some party. All I know is, for the most part, it was empty.

A Memoir: On Love and Life

I had time to kill, because every college freshman in the universe has loads of time to kill. I started surfing the net. It was a public place, so I wasn't looking at pornography (that was for when I got back to my room). I situated my Bible on top of the computer to my right while I scrolled through the screen. I had the spine of the Bible positioned so that whoever walked into the lab could see it. Don't ask me why; God just works like this.

In walked two girls. I hadn't seen them before in my life. One was darker complected, well shaped, and somewhat professionally dressed. She had her hair in a curly style and a bag around her left shoulder that looked like it hadn't been cleaned out in some time. The other, well, she was different. She wore glasses. She was kind of heavyset, but in the most adorable and attractive way possible. I don't recall what she had on, if only because I assure you that nothing she had on matched. That was just her style.

The two of them came in arguing very loudly. Only God knows what inspired so much intensity. As they walked into the lab, I turned around and gave them a glare, not out of spitefulness, but merely out of human reaction. When two people walk into a quiet room essentially screaming at the top of their lungs, you turn around and look, even if they're two of the most tender-eyed people on the planet. (That wasn't the case here, of course.)

I proceeded to check out every sports website that came to mind. Ten minutes had passed, and I was just about done reading about big, sweaty men who chase, dribble, and throw balls for a living. I started packing up. I was halfway through reorganizing my life into my compact book bag when she walked over.

"Ummm, hey," the adorable, heavy-set girl said while fidgeting around with her glasses.

I responded like any reasonable person when someone you've never spoken to approaches you in a quiet computer lab. "Hey."

We introduced ourselves, albeit briefly. The particulars of the conversation are but a blur, if only because it was so brief. Her name was Samantha.

"I see you have a Bible with you, and I just wanted to invite you to Bible study. It's a couple of groups, but we have one every Tuesday night at seven thirty. You should come." She stumbled over those words in the most graceful way possible. Later, after getting to know Sam and after she became one of my best friends on the planet, I found out that she was amazingly nervous at the time. But from the outset of our relationship, Sam proved she was a trouper.

I later found out that Sam and her friend, Sheryl, had spent a good five to seven minutes determining if they would even say anything to me, and an additional two minutes arguing about who would approach me. I'm glad they got that whole thing settled.

Sam gave me some information and told me the location of the meeting. I gave her my word that I would be there. It was a Thursday, so I had plenty of time to back out. Sam and Sheryl and I went our separate ways. I didn't envision seeing much of either of them in the future. I just didn't see weekly Bible studies as part of my plan for college.

When I came to UWG, I *thought* I knew God. I *thought* I had a relationship with God. I *thought* I knew what it meant to be saved, but, in retrospect, I was a lost puppy.

A Memoir: On Love and Life

I had spent the previous two years of high school leading FCA (Fellowship of Christian Athletes) and attending a church near my mother's house. I was one of the faithful attendees of youth group. I was there; sprawled out on a couch that only God knows what had taken place on, every Wednesday night. For about the first two or three months, I only came for the food. Every Wednesday after study we would go to this Mexican restaurant about ten minutes down the road. I just enjoyed being around some of my peers outside of school.

Normally, I would have to be home by seven o'clock. Moms had to be at work by seven thirty on most nights, so I had to rush home from football practice, take a quick shower, and help her tuck my siblings into bed. Most of the time, she had already fed them, so that helped me out a lot. On days when she was too tired to cook big meals for me and Russ or when she just didn't get around to doing it, I would find my way into the kitchen and whip something together for the two of us. That's when I developed my cooking skills. I didn't have much of a choice in the matter. After dinner, I was usually drained. I would try to make sure Russ was in bed every night by nine o'clock.

You can imagine how that worked out for me. He always managed to swindle his way into an hour of extra TV time. I'm weak when it comes to family—so what?

At the latest, Russ was in bed by 10:30 p.m. On nights when I let him stay up late, if I was extremely tired, I would fall asleep on the couch sitting up so as to make sure I didn't stay asleep for too long. I didn't feel comfortable getting into the bed until I knew he was situated in his, safe and sound.

At eleven, I would call Moms, or Moms would call me, whichever happened first. It was always the same exchange.

Moms: Everything all right?

Me: Yup!

Moms: How are the girls?

Me: Just fine. They're sleeping.

Moms: How's Russ?

Me: Good. He ate and now he's in the bed.

Moms: OK. Love you.

Me: Love you too.

This was the daily evening routine for about twenty-four months, give or take a few. I was always up the next morning by

6:00 a.m. My little sisters' daycare bus came ridiculously early, and Moms didn't get home until about 6:45 a.m. on good traffic days, 7:15 a.m. on rough ones.

She would call my cell phone every day at 5:55 a.m. and whisper, "Good morning, baby boy." It was so sweet and delectable. If anyone can make a 5:55 a.m. wake-up call sound soothing, it was my mother. (Emphasis on the *sound* part—it still sucked, but she made it as easy as possible.)

She would always wait about ten or fifteen minutes and then call the house phone. If I answered the house phone, it meant I was up and moving. If I didn't, she would call my cell phone again. Needless to say, her follow-up calls weren't as sweet, but they always got the job done.

In two years of that routine, I only overslept twice. That makes me proud to this day.

I put such emphasis on this routine because that's what it was. It was my life, and I didn't know any better. But Moms, she made lots of sacrifices over the years, the subtlest of which was those Wednesday night encounters.

Often, youth group didn't end until eight o'clock. We wouldn't leave the restaurant until around nine thirty. Sometimes, my mother would take Wednesday off, choosing to have a day in the middle of the week to rest rather than Friday or Saturday, which, of course, would have been more ideal for her.

Other times, when she couldn't get off work, she would have one of her helpers come and look after the siblings until I got home. At the time, this was no big deal to me, but as I look back on it, I realize that every evening the babysitter came was another morning the babysitter had to get paid. Add to that the cost of eating Mexican every Wednesday (not so much on the amount of money you spend on toilet paper or air freshener, just paying the bill), and I now appreciate just how much she contributed financially to my youth-group outings.

In a way, those Wednesday night youth groups helped shape my early theology. I didn't learn much about the Bible or Christianity—not because it wasn't being taught, but because I just didn't pay much attention. I was respectful. I was quiet. I would attempt to be attentive, but I wasn't passionately entrenched in the message. Youth group was a time to hang out, meet girls, talk about sports and music, crack jokes, and eat Mexican food. But God used that time to show me His love and His grace through some of the most loving people on the planet.

Even through all of that—the time I spent at church on Wednesdays and some on Sundays—I never really grasped God. It just wasn't important enough for me to earnestly seek Him. I knew He existed. I had a vague idea of this God most people talk about, but there was no relationship, and there certainly was no understanding of Christian education or discipleship.

So for some strange reason, there I was that day in the UWG computer lab, armed with a Bible and my limited, skewed-by-the-allure-of-Mexican-food theological prowess. I took the flyer Sam gave me and stuck it in the front part of my Bible.

I hadn't been in college for a month yet, which means I didn't know many people, so it made absolutely no sense for me to stay in Carrollton for the weekend. When I was there, UWG was a suitcase college. Kids rolled in on Monday morning and sometimes Tuesday morning, went about their class schedule, studied occasionally, went to whatever parties there were on Thursday, and spent Friday through late Sunday night back at home. It didn't matter how far that ride was, people had no interest staying near the college for the weekend. I never thought Carrollton was *that* bad, but I could see why people would choose their mother's home cooking and sex with their boyfriend or girlfriend who still lived at home over studying in the library and eating a gourmet meal at IHOP.

That weekend, I thought about going to church, primarily because I was inspired by the invitation to Bible study, but I didn't. It was a Sunday in September, so you know what that means: I was glued to the couch downstairs in front of the big screen at Moms's house watching football. Yes, my sin is, and has always been, ever present before me.

The Sermon That Changed My Life

As you can probably guess, I ended up going to Bible study that Tuesday, and the Tuesday after that, and the Tuesday after that. I started building some solid relationships with people who actually believed Jesus was the Son of God and were intent on living their lives in a way that showed that they truly believed. For me, that was encouraging.

That perfect October night came about a month later. I quietly and unassumingly strolled into Bonner Lecture Hall. I sat on the left side in one of the middle rows so as to go relatively unnoticed. I wasn't ashamed of being there, but I did not want anyone to see me either.

I had no idea what to expect. Sometimes, these events could be substantive, informative, and inspirational, and other times they could be flat-out spooky and long. I'm a natural-born skeptic, so I was prepared for the worst. That was probably one of the reasons I chose to situate myself behind most of the crowd, just in case I had to leave early.

About a half hour after the scheduled beginning, Sheryl's friend Awkanba took the microphone. Awkanba was the president and leader of the ministry and one of the top five saved people in the universe that I knew. She was always praying, always fasting, and always leading someone to good works. She provided scripture for nearly every assertion she made. Remember when I said how refreshing it was to see people my age actually making an earnest attempt to live their lives for the glory of Christ? She was one of them—in fact, she was by far one of the greater examples I had.

She welcomed everyone to the program and prayed. Her prayers were long. On this night, it was still a relative shock to me how long and with how much depth and fervency she could pray. I eventually got used to it. It didn't take long. If you were going to be friends with Awkanba, you were going to come to like long prayers, not just expect and tolerate them.

After she prayed, there was a quick worship selection. There was nothing extravagant. We sang maybe two songs, led by a choir made up of two women and one man. There was nothing flashy about it, which is exactly what I liked. I never had a thing for the choirs who make loud noise and orchestrate dance moves and try to prove themselves to be the second coming of Kirk Franklin's gang. I don't knock people who prefer that flavor or style, but for me, I just want some people in complete and total adoration of an awesome and magnificent God. I like having the Gospel in my worship. That's what I got on this night.

The worship leaders concluded and took a seat. Sheryl hopped on stage. She was pacing and slightly out of breath. Once more, she was dressed professionally, and once more, it looked like she'd had a long day. I came to find out that having her shirt halfway tucked in and panting was just part of Sheryl being Sheryl. (Along with so many other things.) She grabbed the microphone and gave the typical salutation. "Praise the Lord, everybody!" she exclaimed.

This is usually the signal to clap or yell with mild to heavy exuberance, so that's what we did. She clapped for a little while longer, wiped what seemed to be a small sweat drop from above her left eyebrow, and proceeded to introduce the speaker.

I had met the speaker a few weeks back. He was a tall fellow with an accent that you knew came from a place with only one high school that had the name of the county in it. He wore regular clothes, used regular words, and ate regular food. He talked about and loved and cared about Jesus, but he wasn't spooky about it. He prayed, but he didn't pray about getting a financial breakthrough or what color shirt he should wear in the morning. He was actually one of the first Christians I had met when I stepped foot on the UWG campus. Richard Paul Martin was his name. Some folks called him Richard. Some folks called him Martin. His rap name was Paul. He introduced himself to me as Rich, so that's what I called him.

I had known beforehand that Rich would be preaching that night, and that was one of the reasons I had gotten out of bed and made my way to the event. The weather had been perfect all day, but there was a storm coming, and I knew I would have to walk ten minutes through the bushes at night to get back to my room. Even so, Rich had made such an impression on me in the month that I had known him that I concluded that hearing what he had to say about Jesus was tremendously important.

As Rich took the stage, we clapped. He grabbed his Bible and a notebook and placed them on the podium. At that point, I figured I would be there for a while, so I took my book bag and jacket off and placed both of them in the seat to my right. To the left was an aisle, followed by another section of chairs.

Rich was getting settled. He was about to pray, but then something dawned on him. I suppose he realized he was going to be there for a long time, too. His first words onstage, as he got ready to preach: "My feet hurt, y'all. I'm bout to take my shoes off."

No objections. He had on black dress shoes with no laces. He had probably been walking in them all day. By the time I left UWG, I knew how it felt to walk in dress shoes for an entire day all too well.

He slipped his feet out of his shoes, grabbed the see-through podium on each side, and prayed. We said, "Amen."

This wasn't your typical sermon. The first thing Rich had us do was pull out a sheet of paper and write down our sins.

He implored us not to put our names on it. When you're in college and you've spent most of the past thirteen years being told you'd better put your name on something or it won't count, you tend to put your name on everything. I managed to follow directions with relative ease this time around.

I wrote my sins down. As everyone was writing, Rich helped narrow it a bit. "Better yet, write down a few sins, maybe five or six, that you *really* struggle with," he said.

That wasn't too difficult for me. Again, I knew I had sins, and I knew I had a bunch of them, but I presumed I was a relatively "good" guy who didn't tick God off too much. I didn't drink, I wasn't having sex, and I didn't do drugs, so in my mind,

God was pleased with me. On that sheet of paper, I wrote down, in no particular order, pornography, cursing, lying, cheating. (OK...pornography was probably number one.)

I just recently came to know pornography as a sin in the few weeks I had been attending bible study. I had made the decision to wait until I got married to have sex again, so in my mind, there was absolutely nothing wrong with pornography. After I started attending Bible study regularly, however, I quickly came to the reality of the scriptures. (No worries, there's an entire chapter on this subject later.)

Rich gave us all about three minutes to write our sins down. We folded the sheet of paper over about three or four times. He had brought along a small basket and proceeded to walk around the lecture hall with it. I don't think anyone knew what he was going to do with them; we just assumed/hoped/demanded that they wouldn't be read out aloud. (I think Sheryl and Awkanba got a little worried for 10.9 seconds that this was in fact what Rich was going to do, but as the eleventh second approached, they calmed down, settled in, and trusted that things would go smoothly. They did.)

Rich got back up on the stage. He placed the basket of sins on the podium, just to the left of his Bible. He took a deep breath, followed by a deeper sigh, rubbed the scalp area of his head to his forehead, clutched each side of the podium with his hands once more, and exclaimed, with passion and curiosity, "Why are you here?"

I'm not sure most people understood why he was asking this question. I don't even know if I initially understood why he was asking that question, or what he meant, or where he was going. He asked it again, this time with a little more clarity but enough ambiguity to keep our minds wandering a little longer.

"Why are you here right now?" he exclaimed even louder. "Why are you in college? Why are you sitting where you are sitting, here at West Georgia?"

I paused. My mind went into a deep rift of thought and tried to come up with the most intellectual response to such a question. I feel like almost everyone in the room tried to do the same thing. Had Rich permitted a few people to share their responses to his question, we probably would have gotten some variation of "I'm here to follow my dreams and make my family's life better," or "College is the gateway and beacon to success and accomplishing your dreams" from 95 percent of the crowd. Whatever words to that effect came out, it would have been absolute hot garbage.

Rich took it into his own hands to help each of us realize the true reason why we were all in college.

"We're all here to make money!" he screamed after giving us about ten seconds to ponder the answer on our own.

Rich was right. We had all become so accustomed to giving some bogus politically correct answer to that question that we had forgotten, in essence, the real reason for coming to college. Behind the fake smiles and crooked compassion we put on from time to time, coming to college, at least for the people who actually left their universities with degrees, college was primarily about one thing: making money. The overall goal of spending four years somewhere and paying people so that you can be stressed and deprive yourself of sleep is the ideal that, once they give you that sheet of paper that supposedly shows you can be somewhat organized, stay on task, work in groups marginally effectively, memorize things long enough to bubble in some answers, and meet deadlines, some company or organization or firm or whoever that can help you keep a car and an apartment and put food in your stomach will recognize that you have those skills as well. In essence, people who come to college and leave with degrees come so they can make more money when they leave. It's the basic premise of a capitalistic society. Sure, you might meet your spouse, and you'll definitely make lifelong friends along the way, but that's not the primary objective.

I think most people were shocked to hear Rich say that, not because it wasn't the truth, but, judging by the facial expressions and the reactions from most of the room, we had all been so conditioned *not* to answer that question that way. From the outset of the sermon, Rich made it OK for us to be brutally honest—not with one another, but with ourselves—about our intentions and about our relationship with God. I think that set the tone for the rest of the message.

Once we rid ourselves of our haughtiness and finally conceded that the primary reason to be in college was indeed to make money, Rich focused his attention on communicating what our primary intention in Christ should be while we're in college, and what our overall purpose, objective, and mission in life should be.

This is where I struggled.

I'm a dreamer. I dream. I dream impossible things, and then I dedicate myself to doing absolutely any and everything it takes to accomplish them. I'm a greater fool. I earnestly believe that with prayer, hard work, and dedication, I can actually change the world. Don't rain on my sunshine.

At the time, however, I wasn't much of a dreamer. I was incredibly unsure about what I wanted and who I wanted to be and where my life was going. I always knew I was coming to college, but primarily because I felt like that's just what you do after high school. I had decided to major in political science and go to law school once these four years had been completed, but that was the extent of my dreams. I had no desire to run for political office. I had no idea what kind of attorney I wanted to be. I had no idea there were so many variations and fields of law. At that moment, I thought all attorneys just studied and practiced law. Needless to say, I hadn't thought this college thing all the way through just yet, so when Rich told us to think about why we were here and how it related to Christ, I was as helpless as a slab of ribs on the Fourth of July.

I had never, to that point, thought about my life in relation to Christ, and fitting God into my dreams, goals, and ambitions wasn't necessarily at the top of my agenda. Rich proceeded through his sermon. He shared a couple of scripture passages and a few more stories about his own experiences before reaching the climax of the message.

He paused for a second and asked someone to bring a trash can up to the stage. He took the basket of sins off the podium, shook it around, and emptied the basket into the trash can. This, he said, illustrated precisely what Christ had done for us on the cross.

Fascinating.

I am sure that was not the first time someone had shown me, in such a practical manner, what the cross *really* meant. I had been to church a few hundred times in my life. Surely someone, somewhere along the way, had painted a picture similar in its practicality to me about the Great Exchange. Still, I guess it was just meant for it all to click for me that night.

The message continued. Rich drew upon that illustration—the fact that Christ had died for our sins and that He experienced the wrath we should have experienced—that He was, in fact, 100 percent man and 100 percent God (the Hypostatic Union), but while on earth he only functioned as man. The love He has for us is far beyond anything these man-made words can do justice to.

That's when it hit me. That's when my life changed forever.

For so long, I had felt God tugging on my heart. I had felt the weight of my sin. I wanted to change and live my life in a way that did nothing but please Him. I desired to serve the Lord and share with others just how good and fateful and awesome God is, but there was always something holding me back.

I am a skeptic. I do not trust easily. I will not open up to you until you have proven yourself. I will believe only 50 percent of what you tell me until I can validate the entire 100 percent. I ask way too many questions. I am sometimes too smart for my own good. (We can sum this entire paragraph up into one word and one sin: *pride*.) These same sentiments applied to Christianity and my relationship with God. I wanted to trust the Lord with every fiber within me, and I wanted to wholly give my life up to His will, His teachings, and His Word, but I felt like God owed me an explanation or, at the least, He didn't deserve all of me because He hadn't given me all of Him.

Russ's disability made me feel like this.

I knew my sin. I knew the mistakes I had made. If I never had the opportunity to marry or have a career or grow old, I conceded that I deserved not to have those chances. But Russ…Russ didn't deserve that, and it wasn't so much about what Russ did and did not deserve as it was about me still wondering and hoping and dreaming and praying. I had all of the usual questions that people who are somewhat intellectual have about Christianity. After all, if you don't think long and hard about dedicating your life to something that claims a dead guy rose from the dead, you're really not thinking for yourself. My issues, points of contention, and reservations—they weren't always what you would expect, though.

That whole being born of a virgin thing? Cool.

That part about two folks eating some fruit they weren't supposed to eat, and that being the reason for the forty-hour workweek, menstrual cycles, unimaginable pain during childbirth, and people having to wear clothes? Fine.

This perfect guy rising from the dead, walking the Earth for forty more days, and then ascending back to heaven, all the while claiming that He is everlasting water and that we can be born again and that love is the most important thing in all the word? Sign me up for that.

I could get on board with all of those assertions. As much as I thought and wondered and was skeptical of those things initially, God tugged on my heart, and as I started reading scripture in its context, coupled that with a better historical understanding of the setting and authors and purpose of each book of the Bible, my faith became even stronger—even as my access to secular knowledge increased. Surprisingly enough, those things didn't bother me. My issue with this whole Christianity thing, the one element of life that kept me from wholly devoting myself to the work of the Lord, was how this

God could send His son to die for our sins and be born of a virgin and walk on water and give blind men sight and turn water into wine and feed five thousand with a few fish and a couple of loaves of bread—but couldn't give a twelve-year-old boy the ability to communicate and share his words like most other twelve-year-old boys. It was a point of contention for me. (As you can probably already tell.)

So what Rich did that night, with that illustration, is show me just how loving and compassionate and awesome our God really is. I have had so many sleepless nights that to attempt to recall them all would be borderline idiotic, but some I remember more vividly than others. I've had my fair share of horrendous nights while Russ weighed heavily on my mind, and for a year or so before leaving for college, I would stay up at night thinking about his eternal security.

Would God *really* send someone who never *really* had the chance to choose Him or worship Him or submit to Him to hell for eternity?

After all, God is loving and compassionate and sacrificial, but He is also jealous and envious, and He pours his wrath out on individuals who openly mock, blaspheme, and reject Him. In my mind, I always worked my way back to the belief that surely God, who, you know, is so loving, would never subject my brother to eternal damnation because Russ would never have the chance to fully recognize God. I struggled with this.

Theological Wrestling

This reality of my life is partly why I have always found it so maddeningly difficult to subscribe to Calvinism and certain sects of reform theology. Do I think that our salvation is entirely bent on us *choosing* to love and honor and serve and worship God? Absolutely not. After all, we're humans, and we're fallible; we are born into sin. We don't know God. What we do know about God, we only know because He allows us to know it. This is why I think it's so unbelievably haughty and arrogant to assert Calvinism as a truth, as part of the Gospel, and not simply as a doctrine. If today's conservative evangelical Christian sect fully believed all five points of Calvinism, but also asserted that some aborted babies go to hell because, you know, some of them just weren't a part of the "elect," then I could at least have a bit more respect for their view. But to say that some people are chosen for heaven and others for hell and that Christ didn't die for all but only for the "elect" while also telling me that aborted babies and imbeciles go to heaven, and then to base that assertion on Romans 1:19–20—well, that's just short of contradictory.

> They know the truth about God because he has made it obvious to them. For ever since the world was created, people have seen the earth and sky. Through everything God made, they can clearly see his invisible qualities—his eternal power and divine nature. So they have no excuse for not knowing God. (Romans 1:19–20 NLT)

So basically you're telling me that aborted babies and people with mental disabilities spend eternity with Christ because they'll never be able to fully see and comprehend and appreciate the complexities of God inherent in the universe? That sounds good. But if you're asserting that they don't go to hell because they never saw or understood the invisible qualities of God in creation, isn't that the same as conceding that there is *some* element of recognition and choice? After all, pro-lifers contend that life starts at conception (and I absolutely agree). And I would venture to believe that over 95 percent of Calvinists are also pro-life. Well, whether you want to believe it or not, that fetus, whether a day old, a month old, or, once born, a year old, is engulfed with sin. She was born into a sinful nature. Sinful parents conceived her. Don't you think God would be right and just and fair to not "elect" that baby in the same way you assert He is right and just and fair to not "elect" Islamic terrorists? You can't have it both ways. Calvinism can't just be a truth when it's convenient to us; it has to be a truth across the board.

I wake up every day by the grace of God. I've been blessed to travel and see the world and be captivated by firework shows and sunsets. I have no excuse, because I can clearly see His invisible qualities, but there's something within my mind, heart, and soul that has to enable me to register and identify with those qualities and relate them back to God in the first place. If the reason for fetuses and imbeciles not going to hell is that they couldn't fully discern the invisible qualities of God, that alone is concession that there is some element of recognition and choice and understanding of the complexities of God and how He chooses to reveal himself in creation and scripture and a host of other ways. When you make something obvious or clear to me, it requires some level of understanding, whether it be through a cultural norm or a certain level of education.

Even people who have never heard about Christ have no excuse for not knowing God, because He has revealed himself in all creation, but there's still a level of choice within that. By saying that people who reject Him have no excuse, you're essentially asserting that these people chose to reject God even though they clearly and obviously saw His beauty in creation. I don't know. I know people a lot smarter than me have wrestled with this complexity. I know you can probably poke a thousand holes in my assertions, in much the same way that if you gave me a week and access to a library, I could poke a thousand in yours. That's just what good intellectuals do. I'm just not ready to make such a wide claim based on a few words from a translation of a translation of a translation.

So I think all aborted babies, children, and people with mental disabilities go to heaven, but I don't think it's solely because Romans 1:19–20 saves them from the "elect/nonelect" status. We don't fully know God. I find comfort in that. Of course you can *say* God predestined and elected us to His calling, because He's God, but that may just be a product of Him being omnipotent. He knows everything. He can do everything. He knows who will wholly and truly serve and worship Him, and he has the power to change anyone's heart, but does that mean He "elects" some and not others? I'm just not ready to make that assertion.

Rich's sermon did a lot for me. It made the all-powerful and sacrificial love of the Lord so incredibly clear to me that the one thing that kept me from God and held me from serving Him wholeheartedly quickly disintegrated. If God would die for me and my sins, failures, and shortcomings, it would be so incredibly haughty of me to assert that the same sacrifice was not afforded to the person sitting next to me in algebra class.

A Memoir: On Love and Life

That evening, Rich helped dispense so many myths, and he showed me just how much Christ loved not only me, but also Russ. That was enough. It was as if my journey to finally make a conscious decision to unequivocally devote my life to Christ was a last-minute, fourth-quarter drive. It started at my own two-yard line, and there were three conversions on third and long and another on what seemed like an impossible fourth and twenty-seven. There were good play calls and bad ones. There was a hold that easily could have been called in the end zone, rendering the entire drive moot, and we might have gotten away with a push off on the second third-down conversion. That doesn't really matter though. Just like in football, you need a few breaks (I call them unmerited blessings, mercy, grace, favor, etc.) that you simply can't control in order to win a championship. During the years of my life that I hadn't lived for Christ, those breaks saved me from having to live with consequences of my sin that would have greatly derailed my life. I can't brag about not having any children or not contracting HIV/AIDS, because I did the act that causes both. It's arrogant of me to look down on any drug user or addict, because, but for the grace of God, the drugs I chose to partake in weren't laced with other, more potent and addictive substances. I experimented with a lot of things that could have permanently hindered, hampered, or ended my life as a result of the emptiness I felt because of Russ's disability, but I know that the Lord kept me under his guidance, protection, and provision in more ways than one, and it is in those provisions that I have since found glory and restoration.

Rich went on to finish his message. I suppose it was very eloquent. I suppose he prayed for many people that night, and that some of those people said some words or made declarations they may or may not have kept. I didn't stick around long enough to know.

Rich concluded his sermon and started to pray, and as soon he did, I walked out. I didn't need any soft music or to see the tears in anyone else's eyes. I didn't need to walk up in front of a bunch of people who knew nothing about me and vow to do something I had vowed to do dozens of times before. I didn't need anyone else's affirmation or adoration. God had spent the past sixty minutes tugging, pulling, and pricking my heart. That night changed my life—forever.

I hadn't known the Holy Spirit as the Spirit before then, or at the least, I certainly didn't identify Him as that. I walked out of the lecture hall and passed the library on the way back to my dorm room and, in that moment, I was a changed young man.

It was the shortest eleven-minute walk of my life. I had on a black jacket that zipped up and some red jogging pants I had always worn after football practice just a year before. I had no umbrella, and the hood of my jacket was about as useful as a fur coat in Arizona. It was raining. It wasn't a light rain, but it wasn't pouring either. It was just right. The rain was falling enough to gracefully slide down the sides of my pants as one leg stepped in front of the other, but not enough to soak my socks and shoes. It provided the right amount of noise in the background as each drop hit the surface of a steel roof or rolled off the leaves that were beginning to litter the ground. In so many ways, that night was fitting. I suppose I could have finally, genuinely decided to live my life for Christ at a church in mid-March, when it was seventy-two degrees and not a cloud in the sky. And after making that declaration, I would go back and hug my friends and family and we would go for Chinese and ice cream afterward. That would be the ideal scenario, or at least the one I thought I would venture to experience prior to actually learning much about Christ. But in retrospect, that was such a stupid vision, if only because I've learned that's not how God works—at least not for me, anyway.

The rain. The song. The message. The walk. The way I felt about Russ. All of those feelings and actions and happenings were so unbelievably fitting for an unbelievable God that was about to take me even further on an unbelievable journey. Following Christ is not easy. It is not picture perfect. The grass is not always greener, and bad things *do* happen to good people. With all that said, I learned that night that the most important aspect and purpose of life is not to make much of myself, but to make most of God. He had designed Russ's disability for a reason. He had placed me in that lecture hall on that campus in that city in that state because he had a plan that far exceeded any plan I could ever fathom. That's just God. I can't explain it, and I won't attempt to.

When the Going Gets Tough

Dr. Turner's office was in the back. You actually have to know where you're going in order to find his office. It's not the easiest place in the world to locate. There aren't many doctors located near his office. I suppose this is for a reason. Much of what we observe is calculated, at least I think so anyway. People try their hardest to make most of what they do—their actions, words, and demeanor—seem unintentional, a relative by-product of whatever emotion they were feeling at the moment. I know the truth, and that's not it. So I reckon if people have that subconscious mentality in them about minuscule, external things, surely a doctor's office carries the same sort of logistical planning. Perhaps I should have known that Dr. Turner only saw patients who had an increased tendency to be volatile. Maybe I should have stayed at home instead of attending the appointment. Perhaps I shouldn't have made my way back home late the night before. Did I mess with Russ's sleeping tendency? Was it something I said in the morning? Did I do something while driving to set him off? Was it simply my presence that made him respond the way he did?

A Memoir: On Love and Life

These are the kinds of things that jolt through the crevices of your mind at 3:00 a.m. while you uncomfortably sink into a not-so-reclining recliner chair in a hospital room that's not intended to house overnight guests. It was early August, and instead of preparing to make the seven-hundred-mile journey to Baltimore to begin law school or spending the amount of time I had left as an intellectually free man playing video games and adding to my movie journal, I was there, sunk into the uneven lumps of one of the most uncomfortable and poorly crafted pieces of furniture I had ever encountered. Adjacent to me, no more than four feet away, was Russ.

I had gotten bored sitting at the hospital since about 1:00 p.m. that day. I hadn't been home to shower or brush my teeth or do any normal, hygienic things that most of us do two or three times per day. There was but one lighting option in the room, so I couldn't turn it on and read a book for fear of disturbing Russ. My phone was no longer fully functional, thanks to Russ having mashed it on its face against the computer desk in his room just a few days earlier. I had just spent $150 too much on a phone, and I had no intention of getting a new one any time soon.

A Memoir: On Love and Life

    I refused to turn the television to anything related to sports. I steered clear of the Internet. I boycotted Twitter, and Facebook had become useless. This was the exact same day as the gold medal game in women's soccer at the 2012 Summer Olympics. My girls (yes, they are *my* girls) were going up against Japan almost a year after we (yes, *we*) had our hearts broken in the World Cup Final. Not many people get second chances, and even fewer get second chances with the redemptive nature of this match, but my girls had earned it. They had never disappointed me. I fell in love with this bunch because, collectively, they reminded me so much of myself. They were resilient and skillful; finessed and yet physical. In a way, I was still hurting from the World Cup loss, so today was going to be a day of celebration like none other. Life, just like sports, throws you unexpected scenarios every so often, and the only conceivable thing left for you to do is shut up and make the most of the situation.

    We walked into Dr. Turner's office. Russ and my mother had been here several weeks before. They altered his medication and started putting into place some measures that were supposed to help with Russ's development. With the school year fast approaching, we were all quite eager for Russ to be able to go back to school, but none of us were as eager as he was. For Russ, I think school was the opposite of what it was for me growing up. I had never found a safe haven at school, at least not until I started playing football. Other than that, school wasn't much of a break from the reality that awaited at home and in the rest of my life. When the soles of my shoes hit the foyer, there was Moms and Pops and their issues, or me still trying to come to grips with Russ's disability. When I stepped foot off the yellow bus at school, it was eight endless hours of jokes about my verticality. One of the first things I learned during this thirty-six-hour day was just how much school did for Russ and his happiness and development. It's a bit of a conundrum.

 I spend so much time fretting about Russ and his disability and some of his limitations, when in all actuality, he's probably more fulfilled and comfortable in himself than my parents and I will ever be able to realistically comprehend. Russ doesn't concern himself with what other people think. If you're annoyed or uncomfortable or caught off guard by his repetitive nature and ability to tell you who the Falcons play in week sixteen a full two months before football season even begins, so be it. It doesn't matter who's around; when a song that he likes comes on the radio, he's dancing and singing along like teenaged girls (and I) do to Taylor Swift, Selena Gomez, and Demi Lovato. Russ doesn't care whom the song is by. He doesn't care if you're irritated or disgusted by the fact that he's picking his nose until that oh-so-uncomfortable piece of an infraction makes its way out. It doesn't matter to him that he sometimes prefers to watch old reruns of the *PowerPuff Girls* instead of the fourth quarter of a tightly contested ball game. Lots of people, places, and things were inspirations in the newfound sense of liberation pumping and throbbing fresh within my veins, but Russ deserves more credit for that than anyone else. He's the definition of liberated. He always has been, and for me, he always will be. This is a major reason why my mother and I really wanted to get him back to school in time to begin his high school experience. Russ is himself at school, and everyone *loves* him. His teachers adore him, the kids in other classes love playing sports with him, and I heard the same thing from so many of his teachers: "You must be the big brother! Russ *loves* his big brother; he talks about you all the time." I always just nodded and acted bashful whenever someone tossed that line my way, but secretly, I relished it. Comments like that make me who I am. At this stage of my life, I'm not fond of yearning for the justifications of others, but those comments always served as some slight level of vindication—like all the sacrifices I had made in the previous years were worth it because someone other than myself noticed, appreciated, and cherished everything I tried to always do for Russ…even if they only grasped the surface of that selflessness. People say they get a lot of their traits from their parents, and I suppose that's often true, but I get most of my traits from Russ. He's made me who I am more than anyone else walking the earth.

So there we were, my mother and me, settled into the chairs in Dr. Turner's office. I was the last one to walk into the room. I closed the door behind me and took a survey of the room to determine where I wanted to position myself. This was kind of pointless, as I would obviously take the seat my mother and Russ were not occupying, but whatever. My mom opted for the two-seater sofa backed against a wall adjacent to the door, so I made my way to the chair with a flamingo-colored seat cushion. It was good enough to get the job done, and anyway, I didn't envision being in that chair more than fifteen minutes.

I hadn't eaten for the day yet. I had arrived late the night before and had failed to wake up in time to scarf anything down. The growling of my stomach temporarily overtook me as the appointment began, but I managed to settle it long enough to focus on the conversation.

Dr. Turner asked my mother about Russ's progress since their last visit, which had been about two or three weeks ago.

"It's getting better," my mother responded.

This was always her response, and it often frustrated me. In all actuality, I never *really* knew if Russ was doing fine or if things were really OK at home, because I never felt that my mother was trustworthy with sharing that information. Sure, I understood why: she didn't want me to worry or be anxious about Russ's condition or the ongoing, never-ending problems between her and my father, but I think she failed to realize that that approach, in some ways, served to alienate me. After a while, I just stopped asking the question, if only because I knew I would get the same generic answer each time.

A Memoir: On Love and Life

That lump sum of emotions overtook me when she started to answer Dr. Turner's series of questions. I briefly questioned my decision to come to the appointment. I couldn't help but wonder if she was going to temper her explanations of Russ's actual behavior simply because I was there. Then, in that instinct, I snapped out of my mind warp and realized I had one advantage at this point that I'd rarely had before: I had been at home recently. I had spent the past few weeks experiencing Russ's ups and downs firsthand. In fact, things had gotten so difficult since Christmas of 2011 that even I was running out of ideas or responses. I didn't know what to do. Normally, Russ's behavioral issues or outbursts were limited to certain people, but when the day came that he was bold enough to hit me with all of the force he possessed, I became convinced that there weren't many people on earth he wouldn't clock if he got angry enough.

What I quickly realized was that my presence, at least on this day, meant nothing. It didn't matter that I was around. Something sparked Russ that day that was beyond my comprehension. Almost two years later, I still can't totally pinpoint it. I wish I could clearly tell the story of what happened:

how he gradually escalated to the point that we had to hospitalize him that night; how he couldn't come home for the next few months; how, that weekend, I cried uncontrollably every moment I was alone. My heart had been shattered to pieces. In Dr. Turner's office, within a mere five minutes, Russ went from relaxing and calm to requiring involuntary treatment. And I was there. There wasn't a thing I could do about it. There was not a word in any language that anyone could utter to me to make me feel any better about it. I felt like someone had ripped every loving emotion from my body and replaced it with a sense of angst, anger, and fear. I didn't really know what to do. So, some twelve hours later, I sat in that chair in the hospital room. I felt the stares from the hospital staff; their self-righteous words and expressions dripping from crevices in their one-track brains. Some things don't have to be said, but you can feel them, and with every dirty look or mumble under the breath, I inched closer to the anger I had buried with my dead self years ago.

  At this time, I found myself leaning on the promises of God more than I ever had before. I want to tell you it was because I knew God would get my family and me through this, or that this was a temporary situation and that I knew the Spirit would keep me lifted and motivated and strong throughout the entire process. I presume all of those things were true. Honestly, however, I had nothing and no one else to turn to. There was no one I was comfortable calling. Whenever I thought about how I was feeling, I wanted to give up on life…so I didn't think about it. Sure, I would look four feet to my left and *see* Russ, but that's all I allowed it to be at the time: a mere physical existence. I wasn't ready to deal with it psychologically or think about what was going on. I thought about the situation a few times, and each time I thought about it, I ended up letting enough liquid come out of my eyes to fill a Dasani water bottle. I was tired of crying, and I sure wasn't about to let anyone know that I was crying. So instead, I sat there, lumped in the crevices of an uncomfortable chair, thinking about a soccer game and keeping faith that this too would pass…eventually.

I Can't Believe I Let Russ Down

A Memoir: On Love and Life

It hurt so bad having my brother trapped in that hospital bed without the slightest idea what was going on or what went wrong. I blamed myself.

I pride myself on being able to understand and work with Russ in a way that no one else can. In many ways, it is one of the ways in which I define myself. I like being good at things. My desire to be successful at anything I do is one of the reasons I don't play card games and loathe playing soccer. Cards and soccer can be enjoyable, but if I don't reasonably believe I can control the game with enough brains and skill, I don't want to play it. As Herm Edwards said, "You play to win the game."

So now that the days were growing longer and Russ's temper was seemingly becoming shorter, I was running out of answers. In a lot of ways, I felt incredibly hurt and grieved by what was taking place. I replayed so many different things in my mind, most of which I had no reasonable control over, but that didn't stop me from questioning every move in my life.

For some reason, I felt like I had let Russ down, like something I had done or a decision I had made had led him to this point. From time to time, in my most intimate of alone moments, I still feel the same way.

People always tried to tell me that Russ's predicament was not my fault and that I couldn't have done anything about it. They always tried to make me feel better by saying I had done more than most people they know would have done. Words like that were never much of a comfort to me. I've always felt a strong connection to Russ, and I'm not exactly sure why. Sure, he's my brother, and I am my brother's keeper, but the love I have for this dude is unreal. I play back a lot of things in my mind, and those flashbacks help me realize why I force myself to be more like a father than a brother sometimes.

I remember one Super Bowl Sunday. It was Super Bowl XL (forty for those Roman numeral illiterates—it's fine; I am illiterate at a lot of things; trust me). The Steelers and the Seahawks were getting ready to play for the Vince Lombardi trophy. I had been going about my usual Sunday routine at the time: sleep in late, ask one of my parents to fix breakfast, take a nap after getting full, play video games, and watch sports. I was a creature of habit, and a string of activities that enjoyable doesn't really need to be tampered with.

Super Bowls have amazingly long everything: long pregame shows; long pregame concerts; long stories about long snappers; long halftime; long, extensive coverage…just plain long everything. Even so, being the sports nut that I am, I indulge in every second of it. In my mind, it's the Super Bowl, and part of what makes the Super Bowl what it is, along with so many other man-made moments of importance and historical excellence, is the amount of time, money, and attention we put into it. I had decided to take a break from the excessively long pregame show and hopped up the stairs to grab some orange juice from the fridge. As I turned on the landing, preparing to place my right foot on the first carpeted step that led to the kitchen, I saw him at the refrigerator door: it was my dad.

Normally, this wasn't an occasion worth noting. My dad didn't invade the fridge with the same frequency I did, but he was like most normal Westerners, so raiding the fridge a few times per day was nothing out of the ordinary. That image alone wasn't enough to strike fear, confusion, or loneliness into my mind and heart; it was the abstract of the photo once I was able to see it in its full context.

As I reached the apex of the stairs, I looked over to my right in the small break in the wall that created a hallway that led to the three upstairs bedrooms. Right by the coat closet door, directly diagonal to the entrance of the kitchen, were a couple of my father's bags. There was even a gallon of water sitting there for good measure. He emerged from within the fridge with a few pieces of fruit and proceeded to inch his way to the counter to slip a couple of rolls of paper towels off the holster. He saw me as his head left the refrigerator and said to me, "I'm going to Maryland. I'll be back Thursday."

Friday morning came slower than a heat wave on Christmas Eve, and lo and behold, that Black Nissan pickup truck hadn't made its way back into the driveway on Thursday evening.

With a straight conscience, I can't tell you I really expected him to be back on Thursday. My parents, after all, had had their fair share of issues throughout their time together. Whenever people learn and grow and experience life in the way those two did growing up, you can expect some growing pains and heartache. Even with all of that, I am not sure I was ever prepared for my dad not to come back, or at least to be so far away.

The writing was on the wall for this occasion for some time. There were lots of moments and memories that led to this exchange at the refrigerator, many of which I am not comfortable divulging within these pages, but they seemed to build upon one another. My parents had disputes and fights, just like all couples do, but my folks argued with a fervency that made me wonder many times growing up if it would be best for them to split up. In fact, as I entered my teenage years, I remember being alone at times—late at night in my room or roaming the neighborhood by myself in my own thoughts—and thinking it would be better for all of us if they split. The confrontations were just becoming too much for me to handle, and the pain of seeing my parents' dysfunction simply served as fuel to my already rebellious spirit. As a kid, you want to see your parents in love; you want to see your dad cherishing your mother's company and your mother doing sweet little things for your father. Don't get me wrong, there were moments I saw and experienced this, but fear has a way of creeping through the senses and outweighing the memories of the mind that are most loving and encouraging. And the truth was, it seemed like the bad moments simply outweighed the good.

    At a certain point, I realized there was nothing I could do about their relationship, so I slowly came to grips with it. I spent a few years angry about it, another couple of years blaming myself for it, another year blaming myself because I told my parents I wanted a little brother, and another year just hating life and wishing I had never been born. I don't think my parents' situation alone made me feel like this, as I am certain it was a compilation of the many struggles endured throughout a childhood that aided in the incarceration and subsequent lethal injection of my innocence, but everything I saw them go through definitely played a huge part in it. And that was only what I actually *saw*.

    So much of this ran through my mind throughout that entire week my dad was gone. I hopelessly wanted but realistically knew that he wasn't coming back—not to live in the same house at least. With every separation agreement or argument or phone call, I held out faith that my parents would reconcile and settle the many differences they had developed over the years. At the time, Thursday was my last hope of this, and that hope came and went without much happening.

I made my way back downstairs and continued watching the prolonged coverage of the game. It didn't mean much to me at that point. I remember Super Bowl XL as the worst Super Bowl of my life, and though I'm sure I am not the only one who shares those sentiments, it ranks so low in my heart for obvious reasons. Russ and I watched the game that night, but without much interest. He went to bed around halftime. I stayed up and watched the game in its entirety. The score was 21–10. Pittsburgh had managed to win their fourth Super Bowl title. Some folks say Seattle was cheated out of the game, that the refs made a series of egregious calls that swayed the outcome in ways that shouldn't happen during a championship bout. I suppose one could make a compelling case for this. All I really remember is watching the Super Bowl by myself. Russ had gone to bed. My sister was off at college and was probably studying her tail off. My mother was probably doing things to start covering the wounds of her heart.

My father was most likely equally searching for fulfillment through his choice of therapy. I just sat there on the couch and watched, and I wondered if I would ever feel that lonely and deserted again.

I suppose this is a big part of the responsibility I feel toward Russ. To want to take care of your brother is one thing, to desire to look after him until your dying day because you never want him to experience the same level of loneliness you felt as an adolescent, well, that puts a different level of weight on your shoulders. Often, I found myself at the altar at church, in the corner of a room with little to no light, staring off into space during football practice, simply daydreaming. I would dream about being at a different place in my life—about what things would be like a decade from now after I had done all the things I kept telling myself I would do. I would wonder how life would be different—heck, *if* life would be different—if I hadn't said over and over and over again that I wanted a little brother. Even so, most importantly, particularly during my college years, I would wonder just how big of a mistake I made going to West Georgia.

Sometimes, I was able to answer that question with little to no guilt, as I found it easy to reconcile my decision with the understanding that giving my brother the life I envision giving him required some kind of college degree. At the same time, the other part of me would continue throwing haymakers and combinations at my already-swollen-shut eye. Yeah, West Georgia was college, and I had to go to college, but why didn't I choose Kennesaw State, which was much closer to my mother's house? As I told myself on numerous occasions, at least I could have stayed at home, and who knows how that might have positively impacted Russ's development during those pivotal years.

    That wasn't the end of my guilt. In the moments when I came to grips with my decision to go out west, I still kicked myself in the gut repeatedly for being so involved. By my senior year of college, I had become student body president, led an on-campus ministry, was training to be a minister at my local church, and had entrenched myself into a committed, long-term relationship. In so many respects, I felt I was robbing something, or someone, of the time they deserved. During the most difficult of times we faced with Russ, I always questioned my decision-making and my overall commitment to him and my family. What if I had dropped even one of those things? How many more weekends could I have spent with him? How many more games could we have watched together? Could I have saved him from whatever so egregiously hurt his heart? To this day, my conscience, in some regards, remains unclean. While I was out having fun, experiencing the whole college thing and trying to find myself (whatever that really means) Russ probably felt lonelier than an infant left on the porch of a nursing home in the dead of winter. I know he was hurt. He had to be hurt. I was hurt. Even so, I felt like I was completely selfish—so incredibly enamored of my desires, dreams, and ambitions that I forgot all about him. Even if it was only for a few months, or maybe even a few years, I forgot what it meant to be a great big brother. I put my duties as my brother's keeper second to being great at life and being a great boyfriend and church member. And while all of those things are important and a source of ministry in their own right, it felt like I had allowed my number one ministry to go to the wayside.

To be fair, it wasn't as if Russ wasn't taken care of or that he didn't have anyone around, because he did. My mother was and still is a heck of a caretaker, and my father always made an immense effort to still be a part of raising Russ. Regardless, it seemed like those times were few and far between. As a result, there are some nights when the only thing I can think about is how alone Russ must have felt on many occasions. How, while I was watching a football game with my brothers from church, he was downstairs at the house by himself: throwing the ball in the air to himself; playing around and tackling himself; talking, cheering, and patting himself on the butt; getting excited about big plays and despondent about letdowns by himself. Those moments should have never happened. I should have been there. I know that feeling of loneliness all too well, and it's one of the most (if not the most) painful feelings on earth.

I Can't

There are so many things I wish I could change. That doesn't imply regret. I don't regret anything, because every decision I have ever made has made me the man I am today.

While I am still laden with an immense amount of flaws, the grace of God has continued to cover me. My life is merely a collection of stories and tidbits that I pray will help someone else not make the same mistakes. I could die tomorrow and be perfectly content with who I am and what I've done. That contentedness is something to find solace in, but it doesn't come without its fair share of nightmares, sleepless nights, and tears. Russ was always such a big part of that pain. Surely, he's the joy of my life, and he always will be. With every decision I make in life, Russ plays a role in the background, if not at the heart of it. Sometimes, that can work to my benefit and sometimes to my detriment—I'm not the jury on that one. I've come to grips with the fact that I can't change what I've done in the past. There's no placing myself at the house with Russ instead of going out on a date with Katrina. (You'll meet her shortly.) It's impossible to go back in time and enroll at Kennesaw State instead of West Georgia. I can't replay every moment of fear and loneliness that plays repeatedly in Russ's head, thus causing him to act out in the way that he does from time to time. Yes, I wish I could change all of these things, but I can't. And I am just now starting to come to understand that it is perfectly all right for me to be helpless. As much I resent myself for many of these decisions, God played a hand in them whether I like it or not. Six years later, I am less prideful and more humble, acknowledging that my abilities are finite; they have a limit; in a multitude of ways, they're obtuse and drenched in deceit and sin. But His ways are perfect—they are glorious and everlasting; they are infinite and beautiful; they spark feelings of open vulnerability and the tug of butterflies in your stomach. I can't explain it, and that's a good thing. You see, if I *had* to sum up what I've learned through Russ in seventeen years in only two words, it would be just that: I can't.

    I can't do the things of God. I can't save everyone. I can't hold myself responsible for Russ's autism or any other medical conditions he may acquire in the future. I can't go back and change time. I can't bear the responsibility of him feeling alone. I can't stay strong for him under my own power. I can't, but God can. There's not much more of an explanation for me.

    I uttered these words with one of my closer colleagues a few years back. He's a skeptic, and in so many words, he told me that my relationship with God seemed like something that was a mere by-product of hurt, confusion, and ignorance concerning Russ's situation. Don't get mad at that statement, because I didn't. In fact, it was a teachable moment for both of us. I didn't offer up an immediate response. Instead, I simply defended my faith and we continued in our conversation. I thought about his viewpoint for the rest of the night and came to the conclusion that, while I could easily see the logic in his thinking, I completely and wholeheartedly disagreed.

In my world, cynicism is an intellectual response, and I've been a cynic far longer than most people realize. God wasn't real to me for the longest time, and during the most difficult years of my life, God certainly wasn't good. He wasn't a friend. He didn't offer any practical or conceivable way out. Words from a book written 3,500 years ago didn't console me when I saw the pain in my parents' eyes about a new diagnosis or overheard the dozens of conversations about potential new treatment plans that could better Russ's condition, only to overhear another conversation some weeks later detailing how much disappointment was inside my parents' hearts when this treatment, too, didn't live up to its promise. If anything, there being no God is still a much easier explanation to me for Russ's condition. No God means Russ's autism is simply the result of chance: a neurological deformity that's the result of a number of different physical or psychological abnormalities obtained at some point from conception to birth. When it comes to issues like this, or the disappearance of a child, or the loss of a loved one, or finding out your new spouse has cancer or can't bear children, chance is easier to accept than God. Even though most people would like to pretend these kinds of things don't happen to them, God makes you angry. God makes you question life. God makes you wonder if He is really good, and if He is, how He could let such a thing happen to *you*. God makes you question all humanity. He makes you ponder the origins of the earth and wonder if there really is an afterlife—if the pain you can't shake is destined to last for the duration of your existence. When life is painful, and you know life may never cease to fill you with anything other than pain, who really wants to spend eternity with God? Is there even eternity? At times, I find myself believing I would prefer an eternal nothingness to existing, in whatever capacity, forever. That's a long time. The thought of being nothing doesn't serve as a source of fear, simply because there's no point of reference. After all, when you become nothing, it's not like you know you used to be something. A part of me would prefer an eternal nothingness to a glorious, eternal presence, no matter who I would spend it with. At least this is how I feel when I think about Russ, because an eternal nothingness truly means that *no one* is responsible. An eternal nothingness means that there is no being out there that *could have* changed the trajectory of Russ's life but *chose* not to for whatever reason. That's what God does. At least, that's what God did for me six or seven years ago. So when people insinuate that my relationship with God is the result of fear, confusion, and imaginative fortitude, I offer them that explanation.

As difficult as things have been, and as easy as it would be to embrace chance over intelligence, the Gospel still serves as a source of strength. I've seen so many lives change for the better when people around me have also embraced "I can't" with their own lives. In the same way that I gave up my desire to have control over Russ's life, well-being, and predicament, I have been blessed to see so many others say the same thing about their past. These people, in many ways, have gone through things in life one thousand times more difficult than anything I have ever encountered. I've seen young women whose first sexual encounters were with an uncle against their will say "I can't" to God. I've witnessed young men who have carried the corpses of childhood friends in so many words whisper "I can't" unto the Lord. Women who have been abused, physically and emotionally, have turned their lives around in ways that acknowledge "they can't" move on from their hurt, emptiness, or loneliness without the assistance of God, without the presence of the Holy Spirit, absent the sacrifice of Jesus on the cross. And because I've witnessed all of these people, and so many more, tell the Lord "they can't," there's no way I can live life without a belief that God can heal every possible pain, bring you through every imaginable heartache, transform every tear into a testimony, or touch the most intimate parts of hearts, permitting us to become stronger and more vulnerable in the process. Russ has taught me that I can't be everything to everyone. That's not a bad thing. While I can't save the world, I can love hard; I can make reasonable sacrifices to ensure that people know I love them; I can do amazing things for people who can't do, and may never be able to do, anything for me; I can dedicate my life to working the purpose God has given unto me. I once heard that the word *can't* should never be in a man's vocabulary, and for the longest time, I agreed with that exertion. Nonetheless, if we *can* do all things through Christ who strengthens us, I think it's applicable to substitute *can* with *can't* if Christ is not at the center of our hearts.

Chapter 3

Love and Life: The Way the Wind Blows

I love my parents. Growing up, my father taught me how to be a man in ways I never fully realized until recently. My mother, on the other hand, showed me what it meant to be a caretaker and nurturer. Make no mistake about it: I believe children function best when in a two-parent household. Now, that doesn't mean children who don't live with both parents cannot grow up to be successful, but it does mean that many of the problems in our society could be alleviated if we spent more time, money, energy, and resources on putting the family structure back together.

I consider myself one of the lucky ones. Though my father was absent for most of my adolescent years, I never had to deal with the pain of not knowing him. Some days, I think him leaving was actually more painful than never knowing him would have been, but I suppose I will never know the answer. What I do remember is, after scoring the only points of my high school football career, shaking my coach's hand, and getting slapped on the helmet by my teammates, I looked up in the stands for my father, all the while knowing he wasn't up there. He was around to lay the foundation, and I thank him for that, but there are lots of things I wish to this day he had been around to experience. That's just life.

My mother, on the other hand, has served as a source of grief many times as well. As a young adult, I often have dreams about my childhood, and I wake up from these dreams in a cold sweat, confronting the realization that I never really had the emotional and psychological freedom that children are supposed to have growing up. Not only did I start raising Russ, I also started raising other children (my foster sisters), none of whom I played any role in conceiving or birthing.

I resented my mother and father for a long time. It was because of them that I was forced to take on the responsibilities of a man far before I was ready. It was their inability to peacefully work through their issues that led to my having nightmares about my ability to one day to be a husband and father. It was their relationship incompetence that led me to essentially raise a special needs child when I was barely out of childhood myself.

All of these sentiments adequately express how I felt for years. Nonetheless, I don't blame my parents. In fact, as I get older, I thank them even more for everything they have done for me.

Obviously, my parents are not perfect. They have an array of flaws and were not very good at controlling their anger, submitting to one another, or letting God do improving work in the other. And, on top of that, I saw and heard *a lot* of things growing up that no child should ever see, hear, or experience. Some of those instances were so bad that I can't tell you, with a straight face at least, that those experiences made me a better person. They did not. If anything, most of the negative stuff I saw my parents deal with explains most of the negative stuff you'll read throughout this book. Nonetheless, even through all of that, I still somehow feel that all of life's journeys have made me a better person.

This chapter is short. It is intended to be. I neglect the details of my parent's relationship because, well, it is *their* relationship. I am not at liberty to divulge the intricacies of their marriage before the entire world (nor would I feel comfortable doing so). If they choose to do it themselves, then it will happen. I write this brief chapter for all of you out there who feel so much hurt, grief, or pain as a result of your parents. Maybe you've never known your father. Maybe your mom gave you up for adoption after a year. Perhaps your parents have both passed away. Maybe they fought a lot, and one of them is no longer around as a direct result of the other's actions. You may feel like you are alone, like no one cares about and understands the depth of your hurt, but I want you to know that I do. I want you to know that someone loves you and cares for you and is thinking about you. I want you to know that someone prays for you every day. I want you to know that it doesn't matter what mistakes your parents made or what they encountered while raising you, you can and will be better. I want you to know that it is OK to cry. I want you to know that it is OK to be angry and want to punch walls for Dad not being around. I want you to know that it is fine to question God's sovereignty every Mother's Day when you miss Mom's scent or embrace. I want you to understand that it is natural to wish you had never been born.

  The funny thing about parents is that they are among the few things in life we have absolutely no say in. You pick your friends and your spouse. You sway toward hobbies that most interest and fulfill you. You design or research your own tattoos. You endeavor to join a career that you feel will give you purpose. Parents, well, they are probably the most impactful people/things in our lives, and we have no control over who they are. None of us ask to be born, and yet we are. Why is that? The answer to that question differs for each of us, but regardless of what the answer is, God ordained you to be created as a direct result of your parents. Wherever they are, whoever they may be, and however they might be doing it, they conceived and birthed you. Yes, they may be a tremendous source of pain, frustration, and hurt. They may fail to be who we expect them to be. They may fail to provide for our basic needs. Whatever your situation, and no matter how low you may feel, your purpose is not defined by the people you come from. God has set you apart, and though your parents may not be the role models that generations to come will emulate, *you* can be. You do not have to be an absent father because your father was absent. You don't have be a showgirl because that's what your mother had to do to put food on the table. You will *not* be a woman beater, perpetuating the cycle of violence, just because you saw your father beat your mother. You will not bring men home at all hours of the night because your dad never showed you how a man should love a woman. That bondage we feel as a direct result of our parents' deficiencies, that doesn't have to be a generational thing. Instead, those negative traits can and will end as soon as we accept the fact that, while our upbringing may not have taken place in the most ideal circumstances, our future will. Of course, this doesn't mean that our future will be perfect or that we will be perfect parents, because we won't. We will fall short continuously, and no matter how hard we try to avoid it, we will disappoint and hurt our children too. Even so, our children will know that they are loved. They will know that there is a God who loves them. They will know that their success is defined by the choices they make.

    In essence, even through all of the things I saw my parents go through and all the despondency I experienced as a direct result of them, they never stopped short of reminding me who the creator of all things good and perfect is. *That*, for all the negative intricacies that life threw at me though my relationship with them, is a true sign of infinite love.

Chapter 4

Life: **The Affectionate Pain**

She was everything to me. She was a marvel. She was a goddess. She could do and see and tell no wrong. Everything about her, well, it was perfect. She was the ideal combination of wits, beauty, and intelligence. Her smile was like no other, her speech swift enough to melt you away. Her hair was radiant. Her smell was exquisite. Her lips were gentle. Her soul was of another kind.

When she touched me, every sense in every fiber of every bone and vessel of my body melted away. It was as if nothing else in the universe even mattered. No one else in the world meant a thing. She…she was everything.

Then life hit once more.

It was the second week of undergrad. I was still an outsider; after all, I wasn't supposed to be there. I had made what had to be one of the most last-minute college decisions in history, choosing to take my talents to the University of West Georgia in little ol' Carrollton, Georgia, over Howard University in Washington, DC.

Why?

Well, I had played a technological game of footsie with the Howard financial aid office all summer. I suppose some of this was my fault. I don't recall in detail how we came to the impasse that we came to, but having two sisters who knew firsthand the ins and outs of historically black colleges and universities, I know for a fact that I didn't wait until three weeks before the semester began to get my financial aid stuff situated.

I was just a few weeks away from making the move up to DC and starting a new life. *Finally,* I thought, *I'm going to leave home, venture out, and be selfish for a change. My life will finally be about me.*

I was in for a rude awakening.

My naïveté was on full display. I hadn't fully grasped the cost of getting an education at the flagship private institution for Blacks. It was the beginning of August, and I'd been calling and e-mailing the Howard financial aid office for weeks asking about my award package, which was finally available for review.

Of course I never got a phone call informing me of this. Nah. Every day, I logged into my brand-new HU account and checked my financial aid status—once at 11:00 a.m. and again at 6:00 p.m. Never mind registering for classes or choosing a major or figuring out where I was going to live—I had to make sure I would have the money to begin with.

That's when reality hit.

I looked under my award status and it read, in so many words, Federal Student Loan: $20,000 for fall; $20,000 for spring.

If you know who Clay Davis[2] is, insert his signature line here…

I thought about the reality of taking out a $40,000 loan for one year of education. Then I thought about multiplying that $40,000 by four years. Then I thought about the added expense of three years of law school that would immediately follow

---

[2] Clay Davis is a character from David Simon's *The Wire*. The showed aired on HBO from 2004 to 2008.

undergrad. I contemplated all of these things and, in one split second, knew I had to make a change.

There were other factors in my mind, of course. My brother was thirteen. He was just entering his teenage years, and the relationship between our parents was extremely rocky to say the least. I wanted to be near Russ. If you've read this far, you know how just how much he means to me. But there were other reasons for staying close to home as well. I was infatuated with this girl. I'd like to call her my high school sweetheart, but I figure you'd actually have to have been in a relationship with someone during high school to claim her as your sweetheart. That surely wasn't us. And by the way, she wasn't the woman I described at the beginning of this chapter. (You'll fall in and out of love with her later.)

I suppose I should take this time to qualify this section. This chapter isn't solely about women. It's mostly in reference to women, simply because most of the people I've built deep, lasting relationships with are women, but that's not the totality of it. Affection and intimacy are most often expressed, and most deeply injured, in the contour of romance, but they exist and flourish in relationships without any sexual connection.

Relationships, more so than money, kept me in Georgia. I just never made the parties privy to those relationships aware of that fact.

So, at seventeen years of age, I was stuck, feeling like a castaway on a tiny deserted island. I had to make a huge financial decision at a time when I didn't even have a checking account. I had other options, but all of them tended to lead to the same end. I had scholarship offers from St. John's and Seton Hall, but they were only partials, and though each school was offering to cover 25 percent of tuition and housing combined, that didn't put enough of a dent into the hole I would dig myself into by choosing to attend a school that cost over $40,000 per year.

I thought about the financial implications of each decision and rearranged my college pecking order: (1) Howard, (2) St. John's, (3) Seton Hall, (4) West Georgia. I didn't even remember applying to West Georgia. I didn't have much in the way of a college search. I mean, I always knew I was going to go to a good college, but the homicidal competitive nature I have in all areas of life now only went as far as the football field back then. If I had really cared about high school starting my freshman year, there is little to no doubt in my mind I would have ended up at Stanford or Harvard. Instead, I spent time chasing girls, playing and watching sports, and napping in AP US History class every day before football practice. I don't regret a thing either, people, not one little bit.

About a week before I had to make the final decision about where I would spend the next four years of my life, lose my virginity, and meet my wife (I wish I was kidding about all of those things, but that's just how your mind works at seventeen), my mother and I hopped in the car and made the forty-five-minute drive out to Carrollton.

It was the worst experience of my life.

Moms had been proactive. She had called and set up a tour and told the people that I wanted to see the campus and some of the available dorm rooms. This was July in the Deep South, so I was more interested in seeing the gym and whether or not the food was edible, not walking around in 100 percent humidity. We strolled through campus, becoming familiar with the gymnasium and other parts I figured I would become quite fond of. The tour was short-lived, a half hour at most. I wasn't interested in coming to West Georgia, so I certainly wasn't interested in walking around a dead campus on a ninety-two-degree day with humidity that feels like you're in a sauna. As we walked back to the car, Moms could see how despondent I looked.

"It's not going to be like this all year. It's early August. No one is here. It will get better, and you'll come to like it. I promise," she said.

I nodded, gave a fake grin, and put my seatbelt on. My decision had already been made. I just needed a little more time to come to grips with it. The short ride back home seemed like an eternity as we passed the exit signs on Interstate 20. I had heard so many stories about West Georgia and knew of so many people who had gone there before me who didn't have the grades I had. Looking back on it, I was prideful and arrogant and haughty; there's just no other way to put it. In my mind, I was simply too good to go to West Georgia. My grade point average was higher than those of some other people I knew who were going there, and I believed my smart-kid reputation in high school would evaporate if I made this choice. It took some time, but I finally wised up.

Two days later, my mother and I returned to campus, this time to register for my classes. A process that should have taken ten minutes took me thirty. I have no idea why. I didn't know any of the professors and I was not aware of the awesomeness that is ratemyprofessor.com. I blindly selected four classes from a list of about sixteen that were required and got a folder that I was told I should read in advance of beginning my undergraduate career. I didn't look at anything in that folder.

So there I was, in my second week at a school that I had no intention of attending. It was a Wednesday morning around eleven. I had just gotten out of my public speaking course and made my way to the campus center. (That's the place with the gymnasium.) Sitting on the couch was one of my good friends, Tunde. He and I had played football together in high school for the past four years. Tunde was a solider, a loyal dude who always had my back no matter what. To me, he was the one who should've never been at West Georgia, because he belonged on a football field in Baton Rouge, Athens, Tuscaloosa, or Gainesville, but here we both were, freshman at this small school in rural Georgia with our whole lives ahead of us.

That's when I saw her.

Tunde had met her first. I think they had one of those big freshman classes together, like biology or English or algebra. If you're looking to get an idea of what ran through my heart when I first laid eyes on her, go back and read the first paragraph of this chapter.

I was mesmerized, and I don't say that simply in hindsight. It's idealistic to claim that you found something when you first lay eyes upon it, only to delay your recognition of this belief until after something materializes years later. That wasn't the case here. Through all of the wandering, I somehow managed to maintain my composure.

"What's up, Lil' Fred!" Tunde yelled in his descriptive voice. I was Lil' Fred in high school, even to people who knew nothing about me. I'm not all that little. Sure, I could stand to be a few inches taller, but four years of intensive weight room training had gotten me to the point where I could bounce 225 pounds off my chest a few times. For a guy who weighed some 80 pounds less than that, that was a big deal. That didn't matter though—Lil' Fred stuck. When you play football, your nickname transcends cultures; it doesn't just get used when you've got shoulder pads and helmet on. Some nicknames are appropriate for everyone to call you. Had I been "Pretty Brown Eyes" Monday through Thursday from 3:30 p.m. until 6:00 p.m. and all weekend, it wouldn't have been OK for anyone else who didn't wear the uniform to call me by my nickname. Lil' Fred was commendable, though, it was something of a badge of honor, a symbol of all the adversity I had fought throughout the years just to be on the team, let alone play meaningful varsity snaps. (And lead the team in rushing two games my senior year, I might add. I'm just saying.)

I responded in my usual reserved way. "What's up, Tunde?" We went on to talk about some topic for the next twenty minutes…probably sports. Our conversation hit one of those pauses that aren't long enough to completely halt the conversation but long enough for each person to wonder if they are being rude. Tunde was being rude. He hadn't introduced the beauty sitting across from him.

"My bad bruh, this is Katrina. Katrina, this my man Fred."

Katrina said hello. It was unlike any hello I had ever heard before, not because it captivated me like a firework show, but because I was in awe of just how rural a hello could sound. You know those movies that blatantly overexaggerate all southern customs, traditions, and notions because the producers are totally oblivious to what life in the South is *really* like? That's how she talked! I barely heard what she had said. I presumed it to be hello, however, and we introduced ourselves to each other. We had surface conversation and asked the general questions that all college students ask each other when they meet for the first time. Where are you from? What high school did you go to? Why did you choose West Georgia? Are you a virgin? (Just kidding.) We talked for a little while longer. Tunde told her how I was a good writer and helped him with all his papers. She seemed ecstatic about this and asked if I would do the same for her. I cautiously agreed. (Because whenever a beautiful woman asks you to proofread her papers for her, you cautiously agree. That's just what you do.) I didn't mind getting her contact information. I figured we would cross paths again or we would connect on Facebook. Then she left for class, and Tunde and I stayed in the campus center for a little while longer. He was always the forthright kind.

"Ay, Lil' Fred, you want me to put you on, bruh?" Tunde asked me with a wide smile on his face.

I chuckled and responded the only way I knew how at the moment. "Nah man, I'm good."

Tunde obliged.

Time passed. Katrina and I did get in touch with each other. We started chatting, on Facebook mostly. It wasn't much. She began e-mailing her papers to me so I could look them over. I didn't make much of it, and in retrospect, there wasn't much there to be made of. I revised and edited dozens of papers for other people while at West Georgia. For a while, that was the extent of our communication. To ensure that I didn't feel like she was using me to help better her English grade, I suppose she threw in an inquiry about me every now and then. I don't think she was using me, and even if she was, she was going to get away with it. At seventeen, when a beautiful woman uses you to revise and edit her papers, you just do it; you don't ask many questions.

Trina and I (The *Ka-* gets dropped once you really to get to know her) started building an actual friendship close to the end of sophomore year. I started hanging around campus more on the weekends, which meant I began attending church more often in the Carrollton area. Earlier that year, Sheryl had started going to a church about twenty minutes away from campus. She raved about how amazing the praise and worship was and how cool the pastor and his wife were. I hadn't joined any church at school yet, so as the crowd went, so too did I. We all fell in love.

Trina had been going to the church her whole life. She became pretty accustomed to the worship, fellowship, and teaching. For me, and for most of the people I hung around, the church provided us with a feeling of belonging and acceptance that we had never felt before.

Some people are privileged because of their family's wealth, status, and prestige. Trina was similar, except instead of loads of money and a house in the Hamptons, she had the picture-perfect, Cosby-esque nuclear family. If you added up all the hours you spent with her, it would take less than two of those hours for you to realize that Katrina Michelle Barlow *loves* her family. I could dig it. After all, my idea of family had evolved in recent years. When thinking about family, I used to conjure up images of a mom and a dad and wonderful, happy, caring siblings. Now, family to me was just anyone who showed interest in me and genuinely cared about my well-being. Trina and I were different in a lot of ways, and it took us a while to recognize it.

As I mentioned, most of our communication was done via Facebook. I would write on her wall from time to time, and she would send me messages about her papers and how it was good to see me at church. She seemed like a pretty good person to talk to and hang out with, so after a while, I started asking her when we could get together outside of paper writing. I always made sure to qualify my request. I didn't want her to think I was trying to make an advance at her, as I figured she was accustomed to guys doing that. At the time, I had a romantic interest in two other girls, and I legitimately thought one had the potential to blossom into something worthwhile, so I wasn't looking for anything substantive. If anything, I had become addicted to the plates of her mother's food that she would bring every so often, and I was intent on doing anything necessary to increase the number of times I was allowed to enjoy her mother's collard greens, ham, and macaroni and cheese.

We started spending time together. We would go to movies and different restaurants. We would talk about everything under the sun. I would tell her about my romantic interests and all the stress they were causing me. She would sit there listening intently, like she was taking notes within her brain, and offer the wisest words of advice she could give at the end. It was a near-perfect friendship. We didn't really know each other that well, but it felt good to get to know somebody without *really* getting to know one another. In retrospect, for a long period of time, we were just friends with one another's representatives. Even so, Trina's representative was starting to cast a heavy spell on me.

I'd Like to Be My Old Self Again, but I'm Still Trying to Find It[3]

I suppose it would be memorable, loving, even borderline romantic to spend an inordinate amount of time reminiscing about the love that Trina and I built—the times we would fall asleep on

---

[3] Lyrics from the song *All Too Well* by Taylor Swift.

the phone with each other; when we held hands as we walked to the car after leaving our favorite restaurant or seeing an awful movie; or the times she would stroke my head as I lay on her chest, with no erotic or sexual innuendo in my mind, just her and me, feeling like the entire world was in each other's arms as we thought about where we had been and dreamed about where we were going. I suppose I could share how I genuinely thought I would spend the rest of my life with her and how the actions I took in life thoroughly began to resemble that. I could even tell you about when she taught me how to tie a tie, or when she held me in a hotel room as I wept about that feeling of still not being "enough" for my father, or the many times I would tell my friends about our timeline to get married. Yeah, I *could* tell you about all of those things, but that would defeat the purpose of this book.

Time went by—it flew by, actually, and Trina and I finally started to get to know each other. We learned each other's likes and dislikes. I learned what ticked her off. She learned exactly how to look, what to say, and what to do to push me over the edge. She knew me. I knew her. We fell in love. It was fast. In retrospect, it was faster than it should have been. Sometimes, life has a cruel way of teaching some of the most painful lessons imaginable, and Trina was one of them for me.

Just know that we were in love, or I was in love with her…or maybe it was that I really loved her and she was starting to fall in love with me. Whatever the case, she had a lot of reservations—she said she didn't believe that a guy who didn't give her half of her genetics could truly care about her with the depth that I did. Physically, Trina was a goddess. There's no disputing that. Even so, physicality wears off tremendously fast, and once you get to know someone else, it's everything except the way they look that keeps you there. There was so much inside of Trina that made her beautiful, and yet so many things about the both of us that kept the relationship from going as far as she and I both dreamed it might. Some moments in life are more distinguishable than others. They are times, circumstances, and situations that, years later, we can look back on and know without any doubt that our life changed at that instant. I haven't experienced many of those. Aside from Rich's sermon and the Ravens winning their second Super Bowl, I normally just take life in stride. That said, Trina was privy to one of those monumental moments.

I remember it like it was yesterday. It was January 2012, toward the end of our senior year in college. The air was cold outside, and I had made the twenty-minute drive up to Trina's house. I loved spending time with her at her house, mostly because of her mother's food (I won't lie to you) but also because I loved her family. I loved the way they interacted with one another. I loved the way they trusted and spent time with each other. Granted, I do believe a certain level of unhealthiness can be present in *any* relationship, and if mothers and daughters can be *too* close, that was certainly Trina (and her sister) and her mother. At the time, that didn't matter to me though. It wasn't so much that Trina had welcomed me into her home—after all, I had let Trina in on everything imaginable about me. What meant the most to me, and what has stuck with me to this day, is the love that her family had for me. They accepted, trusted, and loved me for me. I suppose I made that easy—I was active in my church and about to enter law school while working three part-time jobs.

On paper I was a good bet. Still, I felt accepted, and that meant a lot to me.

So on this cold, early January day, Trina and I were downstairs on what her mother had rightfully deemed our couch. The classification was fitting. No one else ever went downstairs except to do laundry. The basement, for all intents and purposes, was a place for Trina and me to have our downtime. That couch was where she learned my deepest fears and became acquainted with everything that truly is me, and I with her. That couch was special. It wasn't nearly big enough to fit the both of us, but we made it work. I'm not the biggest guy around, and I could barely lie across that couch and not have my legs bent over the side. That didn't matter. Trina and I liked being close to one another. She liked being held, and I did too. Secretly, I think some of her greatest moments were the times when I would fall asleep during whatever movie we were watching, because I always fell asleep and she would still be up, and I think she would stare at me as my head lay slightly above her stomach, my arms clutched tightly around her waist, and I think she would envision us being in that position, *that* interlocked, intimate, and vulnerable position, as long as we both should live.

She had on a long-sleeved gray shirt. It was January, so odds are, even if the heat in the house was set at eighty degrees, she was cold. Trina was always cold. Trina was sitting up, and I was lying down, the back of my head positioned firmly on her thighs. We were watching something, and then we started talking about something. Then, she uttered those fatal words: "I feel like you were living in a fantasy world, like you were moving too fast."

It felt like I was Robb Stark and she was Roose Bolton, her words serving as the sword that pierced through my heart. I was Carrie and she was Mr. Big, and she had decided to drive past the hall because I couldn't locate my phone among the chaos. She was Ray Allen and I was the Celtics, and she had decided to jump ship because she saw the greener grass on the other side. (There, I think I covered most all demographics with those metaphors.)

To put it plainly, those words were like four gunshots to the chest. I don't know what it feels like to be shot by a gun, but I reckon it's an eerily painful feeling, and I assume a number of things run through your mind as those pellets start to spread. Perhaps you wonder if you're about to die, but more importantly, you might start reminiscing about all the things that happened or the things you will lose out on as a result of not being around in the future. You think about your family, your kids, your spouse, or the kids and spouse you want to have and might not have anymore. You might think about all the years you spent in school, only for your life to end at the singular motion of one finger on a nicely constructed piece of metal. A plethora of things could run through your mind, but at the end of the day, it's the finality of it all that runs through your head.

    I didn't realize it at the time, but at that moment, without a long period of healing and reconciliation, Trina and I would never be the same. Our love would never be as all encompassing. Her touch would never be as soothing. Her voice would never be as precious to me. It hurt. It was the most painful thing I had ever experienced. I underestimated just how difficult, and just how long, the recovery process would truly be.

I played it off fairly well. While I acknowledged that her revelation took me by surprise and made me feel a certain kind of way, I refused to be honest with myself. Here I was, a wide-eyed twenty-year-old, dangerously in love and now brought crashing back down to earth. I don't blame Trina for this hurt. In retrospect, I realize that I played just as much of a hand in it as she did. At the time she revealed that we were moving a little too fast for her comfort, I was working three part-time jobs, all the while going to school full time and serving as student body president. I had three different sources of income, and while I was taking care of myself in all regards, Carrollton Junior High was paying quite handsomely. The past few months of my life, twenty hours a week had been devoted to earning enough additional income to put aside into the savings account, all with the intention of putting a nice yellow diamond on Trina's finger sometime in the near future. I don't even think it was just the jobs, though. I had thought long and hard about all the hours I was working. I was still managing to get all As, and my ministerial duties weren't being neglected, so in my mind, even if for some unforeseen reason Trina and I did not work out, I would just have additional income saved up. No biggie.

I guess the real hurdle came in other aspects of my life. Trina never asked me to change who I was. In fact, to her credit, she always seemed to be the more sensible one in the relationship, which in some ways always made me wonder if she really wanted to be in it at all. Every time I would talk about the next phase of life, like where I would go to law or graduate school, she would make sure to insert her infamous line:

"Well, you do what's best for you."

That line always ticked me off. To me, *Trina* was what was best for me. Nearly every decision I made was a calculated one, with her feelings, emotions, and security in mind. As time went on, I started painting pictures in my head. She had stolen my heart, and I didn't want to live too much more of my life without her by my side. At some point along the way, I decided that maybe law school wasn't for me. Knowing that my whole reason for going to college was to eventually go to law school, my parents would interrogate me. They would ask me why I changed my mind, what I planned on doing with a PhD, and whether I thought I could really support my family and have the lifestyle I desired as a teacher instead of an attorney. The truth is, though, they always knew the reason my mind changed. In reality, my mind never had a shift, but my heart did. I had fallen so deeply in love with this woman that I was willing to do anything it took to make her mine as soon as possible. Part of this was me in all of my imagination, placing marriage on a pedestal, but the other part was me believing that this was what Trina wanted too.

    I believed that what I was offering and preparing to give Trina, the way I was prepared to love her, was every woman's dream. It was certainly the dream of every woman from the rural south. It didn't matter to me that I planned to marry shortly after my twenty-second birthday; or that she was my first real relationship; or that law school would be one thousand times tougher to take on at age thirty than at twenty-two. Those things didn't matter to me. Those difficulties didn't register—they were of no consequence and zero importance. Trina was my everything, and I felt it my duty to make sure that she always knew just how much she meant to me.

Perhaps we *were* moving too fast. Perhaps I moved too fast. Maybe things were a little too calculated and my mind wandered a little too much, and maybe I had become a little too fascinated with her voice and her tone and her smell and her touch and her comfort. At the time, I just didn't know any better. I had dreams. I knew I wanted to go to law school. I knew I wanted to be an attorney or a public servant. I knew I was called to serve in the ministry. I knew I wanted to give back to my community and dedicate my life to children and the poor and less fortunate. All of those things, they were dreams, and those dreams remain. But every day I woke up and thought about Trina—and I would see her, look into her eyes, and grab her waist as she wrapped her hands around my shoulders…and, well, that was my most vivid dream. That was the dream I wanted more than anything else. I wanted that moment to last forever—to be one we still relished at sixty-two, after our bodies wrinkled and our health deteriorated.

That's what Trina did to me. She made me dream about situations I never thought I would dream about. She made the future real to me, because every time I gazed into her brown eyes or kissed her soft lips or wrapped my arms around her waist, I looked into the eyes of my future. I was kissing the only lips I ever wanted to taste; I held the only person I ever wanted to dream of holding. Perhaps I should stop writing this now, because I remember all of these emotions a little too well.

The next few months were trying. I'm a stubborn guy, so rarely if ever did I let it be known just how I was feeling inside. Despite the pain I was feeling as a result of our relationship, which stemmed from much more than just that one comment on the couch, I made a conscious decision that I wasn't going to let those things affect me—that this wouldn't be the end of our relationship. I was determined to get past the way I was feeling and work things out with Trina, and all those things she and I had talked about doing so often would come true. Unfortunately, as much I wanted this to be a reality, it just wasn't meant to be.

Time Won't Fly—It's Like I'm Paralyzed by It[4]

---

[4] Lyrics from the song *All Too Well* by Taylor Swift.

Suddenly, I felt like I had enough. It seemed to all come crashing down on my shoulders at once, and maybe I just wasn't strong enough to handle it. I don't know. It all seems somewhat irrelevant now. Things between Trina and I changed drastically. In February of my senior year in college, I made a last minute decision to take the LSAT and go to law school. I was back home for my first winter break during my legal education, and I was exhausted. I was drained mentally, obviously, but that wasn't even the most trying part of my existence the entire semester.

When I made my way up to Baltimore for law school, Russ was still in a facility, and though he had long since checked out, I couldn't help but be constantly consumed by his well-being. There was never any doubt in my mind that he was well taken care of. Still, I lived in a perpetual state of anxiety, always wondering how he felt. I was always wondering where his emotions were. I couldn't stop thinking about how my mother was feeling or how hurt my dad was. My mind would think about if my parents would ever be able to get their stuff together for his sake. I'm still searching for answers to those questions.

A Memoir: On Love and Life

I got home early in the evening on the fifteenth of December. It was an eleven-hour drive, and I had left at about six o'clock in the morning. I had intended to leave much earlier, around eleven o'clock, but I decided to drive during the day instead. My mother's birthday is December 15, and I was determined to make it back home in time to at least kiss her on the cheek and tell her how much I loved her. I made it in time to do all of these things. I'm a boss.

The days went by, and it was December 21. I had been home for almost a week, and Trina and I still hadn't seen each other. I can't say this upset me. A part of me wanted to see her, but a part of me didn't. A part of me was excited about lying under her for the next month, and the other part of me just wanted to see my boys, play with my niece, hang with my family, and help my mother around the house. To be candid, Trina started feeling more like a burden than a treasure, and that was something I never intended.

I had been debating for months whether or not I wanted to break it off again. We broke up for the first time in April of my senior year of college, and I knew this wasn't a decision I could make overnight. If I uttered those fatal words once more, I knew we were done for good. That's just the kind of girl she was, and heck, I can't blame her. If someone broke up with me twice, I'd probably permanently kick her to the curb too. At this point, as it had been for months, Trina and I just weren't seeing eye to eye. Russ's behavior got worse, and my mother was working at night, so I was at home, doing everything I could to try and calm him each night of the week.

It was draining. It was exhausting. It was emotional. It was just something I didn't really feel like talking to Trina about, and since it was the most pressing thing on my mind at the time—what I thought about when I ate, slept, bathed, and watched commercials during football games, I just didn't want to be around her.

Some time before, maybe seven or eight months prior, Trina and I had had a conversation. I don't know how it started, because in retrospect, that's all irrelevant. What matters are the words I remember most. We had been talking about marriage for quite some time. Vaguely. I didn't know if she was serious about it or not, but the fact is Trina didn't seem to get serious about marriage until after I took my talents to Baltimore. Before then, I was living in a fantasy world and moving too fast. Pack your bags and move seven hundred miles away, and suddenly a woman starts texting you pictures with her name signed in cursive and your last name attached. Fancy that. (But I digress.)

In all of this marriage talk, I started being more candid about certain things I think people who are thinking about getting married should talk about. For me, the number one conversation I needed to have, outside of my ministry, had to do with my little brother. Trina had seen everything. She had seen me at my lowest and also at my best. That was the same for Russ. She knew how loving, charismatic, and sacrificial Russ could be, but she had also experienced firsthand the difficulty of taking care of him. It should have come as no surprise that she felt like it shouldn't be my responsibility to look after my brother as long as both my parents were able to do it. We went back and forth about how I wanted Russ to live with me once I completed school and how, for so many reasons, she just wasn't quite up for that. I wasn't sure how to feel.

On one hand, Trina's concerns were valid and legitimate, and I had to take into consideration how she felt about such an arrangement. On the other hand, I was baffled. As much I could see how it would likely make her weary or uncomfortable at first, I couldn't help but think about what would happen if the tables were flipped. Remember, if you recall nothing else about her, note that Katrina Michelle Barlow loves her family. In my mind, if something happened to Trina's sister, there would be no discussions, no sit-downs, and no questions—we would simply adapt our lives to fit the needs of her sister. And to be totally honest with you, I wouldn't mind that. I would embrace it. I think that's what life and marriage and family are really about. For many reasons, Trina didn't feel like that was something she was capable of, at least not with Russ's predicament. I tried to stress that by the time we actually tied the knot, Russ would be doing much better, and I wouldn't move him in with us until I was able to make him his own space with his own kitchen and his own bathroom. Perhaps this was a pipe dream of mine, an unattainable illusion that I couldn't properly explain because I couldn't actually envision it myself. Who really knows?

So with all that was going on with Russ, my immeasurable level of exhaustion and months of consideration, I matured a bit and did what I should have done five months earlier. I finally broke it off. Again.

Dear Trina

Fast-forward a few months. We were both still in love with each other. We both had so much invested, so many hopes and dreams for our relationship, that we didn't want to let it go *that* easily. I'm tired of writing about this, primarily because it's one of those things I'm tired of dealing with and I've finally actually moved on; and there's no way I could even remotely begin to articulate my feelings for Trina better than I did in the letter I wrote her:

OK, I know you're probably like why is this guy e-mailing me and what more could he possibly have to say to me? I get it. And with that said, I will make this as brief as humanly possible. The same way you say you put your feelings best down on paper, I do too.

(Or on the computer screen, whichever one truly works.)

A Memoir: On Love and Life

If it's too soon to deal with this, don't read this, because it's long. But this is just me bearing my heart and being honest, absent all of the emotions that accompany a phone call or text. (Writing helps me REALLY express how I feel without the emotional blur.)

Let me start this off by saying, once again, I am so incredibly sorry. I never meant to hurt you. I never meant to do anything to you but love and cherish you for the beautiful queen you are. I've made a lot of mistakes along the way, in my personal life and in our relationship, but I can honestly say that I am starting to grow from all those things. I am becoming a much better man. Much firmer in the things of God. Much more equipped to battle the world with the Spirit rather than the flesh. Better able to fight and overcome temptation. I'm sinful. I will always be sinful. But I see God starting to work in my life in ways I am excited about. And so, I am sorry.

I've given you a few reasons why I felt we should break up. They were all true. If I had to break it down into percentages, 25 percent was the stuff with my brother. But the other 75 percent, well, I guess I'll just have to hash it out.

Let me say this...I LOVE YOU, TRINA. I love you with all of my heart, all my mind, all my body, all my soul. I love you in ways I never thought I would ever be able to love anyone. You're a queen to me, a goddess, and I cherish you. I want to marry you. I want to have children with you. I want to get up at 6:30 in the morning to go to work for you. To take care of you. To make sure you're happy. To make sure you can go to all the places around the world you've ever dreamed of. To give you the life you want to have. I want to be the guy you tap on the shoulder when you're six months pregnant and it's 2:45 in the morning asking me to go get Popeye's chicken and strawberry cheesecake. (Or whatever craving you're having.) I want to wait on bended knee at your very request. I want to fall asleep and wake up to you every day for the rest of my life until I die. I want to grow old with you. I want to come home to you. I want to honor and love you like Christ loved the church. I WANT to do all of those things. I know I may have said them before, but I mean it, I really do.

With that said, we both have A LOT of things to work on. We've acknowledged the things that I'm not so good at. I'm not always good at compromising. I'm not always good at communicating with you. I'm not always good at helping you understand my point of view or what I'm going through. I have a lot of issues, mentally, psychologically, emotionally. I know I have a lot of baggage, and I'm working on it. I am sincerely working on it for myself. And in the back of my mind, whenever God is done bringing me out of this valley, I hope I'm with you and able to love you even harder than I did before. But Trina, I have to be completely honest. I'm scared of a few things.

I know what type of house I want to have and the kind of lifestyle I want to live. I will always honor, love, and cherish my wife above all earthly things because that's what the Bible says to do. My covenant will be with my wife, and I will do everything in my power to make sure she is happy every step of the way. But I'm scared that we just don't see eye to eye on some crucial things. I understand compromise. But when I think of compromise, I think of compromising on how much money we spend on food or entertainment, what kind of vacations we take, what kind of house we'll live in, where we will live, how many children we will have, how much money you spend on SHOES! That's compromise to me. Now, don't get me wrong and don't get mad, I understand where you are coming from. I know you have fears as well and you are scared of some things too. And I respect that. I more than respect that, I acknowledge that. I want to be sensitive to those things because your fears and your desires are just as important as mine.

But Trina, I want us to be a couple that's all about the things of Christ. I'm not saying we weren't. Of course we make mistakes, everyone does, but I want people to look at us and know that we serve Christ. That we represent Christ. That we cherish Christ above all things. I want people to look at the way I treat my wife and see me ministering. That's how prepared I am to love my wife, whoever she is. And to me, that stuff means having an open household. It means taking care of my brother. Heck, to be honest, it means one day taking care of my parents if need be. Not putting them in nursing homes or anything like that. It means that when somebody—your friend, my friend, whoever—needs a place to stay, or a hot meal, or just a conversation or shower, they can come to our home and experience the love of Christ. That is so important to me because that's the love that so many people have shown me. That's the love God has shown me. That's the love God has shown you. And I want the woman I create a covenant with to WANT to share that same love as well.

I know it can be difficult to grasp. I know there will be times when neither of us wants somebody over. I know we'll both be inconvenienced time after time after time. I know we'll invest in a lot of people who will flop. We'll trust a lot of people who will hurt us. We'll do right to a lot of people who will do wrong. I know these things. These things scare me too. But they are things that I have been called to do. I can't run from them if I tried. The only thing that is going to make it possible for me to be the minister, attorney, preacher, politician, etc. that God truly wants me to be, aside from the Spirit of God, is an amazing woman of God, willing to go through everything I go through. And so far, you have been that woman! You have been amazing to me. You have loved me through so many things, seen me in my most vulnerable states. I've allowed you to see me in ways I never wanted to let anybody in. That's one of the reasons why it's so hard to let you go. I know I don't know anybody else the way I know you, and quite frankly, I don't want to. But Trina, I just hope you can understand my point of view. I hope you can come around to seeing why I think the way I do about some things.

Trust me, if something happened to Calia [her sister] tomorrow, she would be more than welcome into our home with open arms. If I had to take a second or third job to help take care of your sister while you were at home all day looking after her, I would do that with open arms, because I would know that at the end of the day, I'm going home to the most amazing woman in the world. A woman who puts the things of Christ above all else. I am NOT saying that you don't do that now, just making a point. My willingness to look after my parents if that day ever comes doesn't end with my parents, I mean that for yours, too. Our house is your friends' house, too. If anything ever happens to your friends or your family, our home, our space, our love is theirs too, because that's what God has called us to. Obviously, I'm not gonna let people run over my wife and me, or mooch, I just desire that we always remember the grace that God has given us, and that we extend that to others. I'm not saying that there won't be days when I would be frustrated. There will be. There will be days when I would come home and just want to watch a movie with my wife, but someone may need to talk to her, or talk to me, or hang in the living room, or use the computer, or whatever it is. In those moments, I hope to decrease in myself and my selfishness and use those moments as opportunities to continue to point people toward the things of Christ.

What scares me most is I don't know if you REALLY want that. And you know what, that is absolutely fine! Honestly. You deserve to have the man, the life, the lifestyle you want. You've earned it. You are beautiful and intelligent and deserve all of it. But Trina, I get concerned sometimes. I get concerned sometimes that you're not involved in church. I get concerned sometimes that it seems like you get disinterested in church, like it's only about the message or whatever. Look, I know you've been in church a lot longer than me, so you see things in a different light. You've known people decades longer than I have. You've interacted with them in ways I haven't. I understand all of that. I know you love Jesus. I know you're saved. I know you desire to live a Godly life and have a Godly husband. I know all of these things, so please don't get angry or take offense. I think we have both earned the right to be completely honest with one another about EVERYTHING. But I got excited when you got back on the praise team. Like you have no idea how excited I was; then you stopped. Same thing with the sound booth. I know these may seem like small things, but with me knowing ministry is going to be such a vast part of my life, I have to know that the woman I tie my soul to is OK with that. Like 100 percent OK with that. And it scares me not to see you involved. It scared me that the first thing you said to me (when I got done preaching) was that I went on too long. But whoever I marry has to understand that that's not me up there. That's not me being long-winded. That's not me spending all my time at church. That's not me inviting everyone over to the house. Heck, that's not me loving her like Christ loved the church; or taking my daughter out on dates; or teaching my son to tie a tie; or looking after my little brother. That's God. And I have a responsibility to continue to do those things. People were weeping; that was God. That's His glory. His majesty. His sovereignty. His will. I can't control that. I say all that to say that the things above, I can't control those either.

What I can control is how much I love my wife. How much she knows I love her. How much I confide in her. How much I open up to her. How much I cherish her. And I plan on making sure without a doubt that she knows I love her more than myself. That I will die for her. You know me. You know how I feel about this stuff. I guess I'm saying that I'm working on me. I'm doing everything I can to make sure I'm a fantastic husband, father, brother, attorney, politician, preacher. I'm not there yet. I will be, but not yet. And what I'm saying is, when all this smoke clears, I want to be that fantastic husband to you. I want to be that amazing father to your children. But you've got to be OK with who I am, and who and what God has called me to be, and the family He has given me, and the people He has placed in my life.

A Memoir: On Love and Life

I'm not asking to get back together right now. I'm not asking you to understand how to respond to this. I hope I don't anger you. That's not my goal. I love you so much. If I didn't, you wouldn't be reading this right now. I'm 600 miles away, I haven't seen you in a month. You know this isn't fluff. This is how I really feel. I want you to be OK with these things, but you have to WANT to. And if not, I totally understand. But with everything we've been through, I truly hope to place a yellow diamond on your ring finger one day. We'll see where life takes us. Like Obama said in his DNC speech, "So now, we have a choice." LOL

I love you! Always have. Always will. Forevermore.

Well, you can guess how that turned out. Such is life.

Chapter 5

Love: **Don't Waste Your Heartache**

It's an understatement to say I learned a lot from that experience. When I was writing this, I took a considerable amount of time between the conclusion of the last chapter and the beginning of this one. Why? Because I wanted to make sure that, emotionally, I was able to present the material in this chapter in a way rooted in scripture and hope, not frustration and resentment.

I can say unequivocally that I have moved on from Trina, and if you've read up to this book, you should know by now that there isn't a single lie in here. That's not to say this emotional liberation happened overnight, because it didn't. There were a lot of restless nights, some days wondering "what if," other days reminiscing to the point of numbness, and a whole lot of prayer, Taylor Swift, and late-night calls to my pastor to help me work through this. All of those things are relevant. Even so, through all of the months that went by between initial break-up and actual detachment, I was unable to free myself from those shackles until

I totally and completely depended on God to help heal my broken heart.

I know it sounds like a cliché, and I know it sounds supersensitive, but it's one of the many truths I've come to know over the course of my short lifetime.

You met Trina marginally. Perhaps these pages do her justice, and perhaps they don't. They may or may not paint a holistic picture of who she is and who she was to me and where our relationship was headed. I can't make that determination. At this juncture, I want people to see the mistakes I made and the things I did right, and apply to them their lives. In my mind, the deterioration of our relationship wasn't anyone's fault in particular. As I look at it from a subjective standpoint, we were just unequally yoked. Strange concept, huh?

If you've spent enough time in a church that minimally teaches the Bible, you've heard this phrase. If you're considering marriage, casually dating, or merely listening in on sermons, conferences, or message boards that talk about courting or marriage, you've heard this phrase before. Even if you're familiar with it already, let me refresh your memory:

> *Don't team up with those who are unbelievers. How can righteousness be a partner with wickedness? How can light live with darkness? (2 Corinthians 6:14 NLT)*

If my relationship with Trina taught me nothing else, it taught me a more meaningful definition of this verse. At first glance, it seems as if Paul (the writer of this letter to the church in Corinth) is instructing us not to hang out with unbelievers. If he says not to spend a considerable amount of time around people who don't believe that Jesus is the Son of God (and have a lifestyle that reflects that belief), then surely we shouldn't hitch our souls to a man or woman who doesn't share that same belief system. But while all of that is true, the two years I spent with Trina taught me something of more considerable value as well.

In that verse, Paul is not encouraging us believers not to spend time with or hang out with unbelievers. If that were the case, it would be pretty tough for us disciples to make more disciples. The task of growing the kingdom of God would be, at best, a daunting one if we were to have *zero* fellowships with unbelievers. Instead, Paul is encouraging us to refrain from prolonged personal and business relationships that could cause us to compromise or sacrifice who we really are as followers of Christ. So when Paul says don't team up with those who are unbelievers, I think he's saying don't go into deep, emotionally binding relationships with people who could cause you to dim your light for Christ. Our relationships should point us to the cross. The company we keep should help increase our salt to the point that we are bitter to a world full of darkness, so bitter that their taste buds conform and they come to know Christ as the sweetness he is to us. That's the goal. But in further study, not so much from a concordance or conference message but instead from simply living life, I've found that being unequally unyoked isn't simply a consequence of forming relationships with people who openly reject the message of the cross.

    Trina and I were unequally yoked. Period. I'm not sure there's any other way to put it. Perhaps I could spin it as us being spiritually incompatible, and that may be a better way to put it, but either way fits the bill. Don't get me wrong—in no way, shape, form, or fashion am I saying that Trina was not saved, nor am I saying that I loved God more than she did or that I was further in my walk with the Lord than she was. I am refraining from claiming any of those things. What I will state without hesitation is that we just weren't on the same page as far as ministry goes. We couldn't agree on what ministry meant; on what a life devoted to God would be like; on what we would be willing to sacrifice for the sake of the Great Commission. There's no problem with those things. I am almost certain there will be times of disagreement about all of the things I just mentioned when I actually do get married, but I will caution any and every young person against marrying someone who already has reservations about your ministry.

When Trina and I were in the latter part of our relationship, one of my better friends offered up some sound words of advice: "A chick with no commitment to ministry gets no commitment at all."

Let me qualify that statement. If I weren't called to the ministry, and if I knew my purpose did not include speaking, preaching, teaching, writing, and potentially pastoring, Trina and I could have gotten married, bought a house in the country thirty minutes away from her parents, had four or five kids, and lived a wonderful, happy, and long life together. I venture to think that she will bless some man with all of those things one day, and he will have earned it. He will have loved her sacrificially, like Christ sacrificially loves his church. But as much as I wanted those things, that particular roadmap just wasn't part of the plan God had for me.

Trina's ministerial commitment may end at serving in the media booth for the next forty years. There's nothing wrong with that. The church is a body, and every media member is a valuable part of the body of Christ. I know this too well. The CDs I received from home during my first semester of law school are what kept me from jumping off bridges and sleeping with prostitutes. I mean it when I say it is a valuable and vital part of the ministry. With that said, the level of commitment needed for her ministry may not be the same level of commitment needed for mine. Preachers and teachers, those preachers who actually fear and love God and take the New Testament literally, know the weight and responsibility of teaching God's Word, and their job is a never-ending vocation. There is no time off. There is no vacation. You are always on call. You must always be in prayer. You must always be equipped with the sword. You must be ready to suffer. You have to be ready to counsel a couple who just lost their six-year-old son in a car accident, or grieve with the newlyweds who just found out they are unable to have children, or mourn with the teenager who came home to find his forty-year-old mother passed out in the bed, lifeless, because she fell back into her drug habit. This occupation, well, it isn't an occupation—it's a way of life. It *is* life. There is no on and off switch, and that means the level of commitment required to do it effectively is much more than two hours every Sunday. It is twenty-four hours a day. Seven days a week. Three hundred sixty-five days a year. Until you die. Let that marinate. If you're thinking about becoming a preacher or teacher or serving in pulpit ministry in any capacity, you need to seriously pray and fast and seek the Lord on it. If you've already done so, pray, fast, and seek the Lord on it some more. You can never be too sure. I would say take this with a grain of salt, but if you take nothing else from scouring through these pages, please take my word that this is not a job you willingly pursue absent the guidance of the Holy Spirit. This is me offering this advice at age twenty-two. Only God knows what more I will encounter, experience, and suffer through as a result of the ministry in the next five or ten years, let alone the next thirty. Take heed to this, then, and make sure you do everything under your power to create a covenant with someone who shares the same level of commitment to the ministry that you do.

This is not a narcissistic way of thinking. If it comes off that way, I sincerely apologize. That is not my intent. As a preacher, it is imperative that my covenant be with someone who shares my commitment to the ministry. That doesn't make women who haven't been called to that any less women of God, and it doesn't make wives of pastors or ministers or politicians "better" women either. It's about ensuring that we do everything we can on the front end to make sure that our lives together as husband and wife are as fulfilling and meaningful as possible.

For so long, I thought there were only two requirements for my marriage: (1) that I marry a woman and (2) that she be a Christian. In the grand scheme of things, those are the only two essentials, but if I desire to live the life and fulfill the purpose, mission, and vision that God has for me while I walk this earth, it is imperative that I tie my soul to someone who is going to make fulfilling those things as easy as possible. It's possible to be an unequally yoked Christian couple. Evaluate your relationship, and if need be, ask the Lord for the strength to terminate it before it's too late.

Emotional Maturity

So what do I mean *by don't waste your heartache*? It's an interesting concept, right? For me, not wasting my heartache meant having the courage and forcing myself to sit down and write this book. Not wasting my heartache meant having the emotional maturity and stability to know that reopening so many wounds—some healed, others scabbing, a few still gushing—may have its cons, so I needed to make sure I was in a good place spiritually before trying to record these events. With all that understood, I can unequivocally say that the situation I so vividly recount, the fairytale days and the ones I would like to have never encountered, they all serve a purpose; they are a part of a grander scheme that I honestly don't know everything about right now. And I think that's OK.

A Memoir: On Love and Life

I think that wishing something had worked out differently, briefly reminiscing about the things you could have done better, and then letting it go and vowing to learn and grow and mature from those situations is healthy. It's liberating, refreshing, and restoring all at once. Of course, this kind of reflection takes a keen amount of maturation and caution. On one hand, you can't allow the past to consume you to the point that you sulk in it, hoping and wishing for third and fourth chances that will never materialize, thus keeping your heart, dreams, goals, and ambitions in neutral without any sensible idea of where you're headed and why you are who you are. In contrast, there's so much to learn about love and life while looking through the rearview mirror. It's not about living in the past or allowing the things behind you to control you. It's much like driving a car. You spend an overwhelming amount of time looking forward, planning for what's ahead and taking note of things that you are currently experiencing and passing while also switching lanes and preparing for upcoming turns and stoplights. You must always be alert, because so much of it is, ironically, not about you and your ability to direct the automobile, but rather about how you're able to respond in moments that are simply out of your control. All the while, you intermittently take a glance out of your rearview mirror, scanning the traffic, figuring out whether that's a cop or a regular ol' Dodge Charger behind you, and exploring the possibilities that may come if you choose to brake check the idiot tailgating you while you're already going fifteen miles over the speed limit. Life, and the lessons that come with it, is much the same.

    The past, or what's behind us, helps us understand what's in front of us—where we're going, how much work is left to be done. The past helps us draw strength from the adversity we have already overcome, while preparing to combat our emotional valleys and tactical mistakes and turn them into testimonies and opportunities for greatness. Life is full of tailgaters, people who annoy us and add little positivity to our lives, but they soon pass. Sometimes, we graciously roll over to the right lane and permit them to continue ahead; other times, we remain stubborn, waiting for them to grasp the idea that we're not moving and have no interest in caving in to their bullying. Regardless of how that brief relationship comes to an end, it is just that: brief. When you realize that there is, in fact, a cop behind you and you are definitely twenty miles over the speed limit, the heart drops, your stomach tangles in knots, and you hesitantly flip your signal and caution lights on as you prepare to be pulled over. And you know he's going to ask you if you want him to check his radar gun to see if it's working again. And you'll say yeah, even though you know you were flying and qualify for a major speeding ticket. But as upsetting or inconvenient as these circumstances are when they happen, we gain something meaningful from them.

A practical part of growing in maturity is application. For example, if I know I really can't afford a $140 speeding ticket right now, I probably shouldn't be driving twenty miles over the speed limit, and in the event I do, I need to be prepared to face the consequences. Such is life.

I am not the same person I was two years ago, and I am more than comfortable in my assertion that I will not be the same person two years from now that I am today. That's natural and fitting. When Trina and I got together; when Russ's disability became more apparent; when my parents had their issues; and when I was preparing to go to law school, I didn't quite know how to respond to any of them. And though only one of those was really under my control, I've realized that how we respond to things we can't control shapes our character so much more than our response to the things we can. As the days progress, I find it easier to deal with the things that come as a direct result of my own stupidity, if only because I have some pretentious belief that I deserve the emotional, physical, and psychological torment that comes with my inability to be patient. Life isn't fair, and in a way, I don't think it should be. I'm not sure what kind of person I would be had my parents been corporate attorneys or my uncle left me a trust fund. In actuality, I'm proud of my struggles. I embrace my sufferings; I relish my tears. Those things have made me who I am; they've helped me find myself and the things that are of most importance to me. I concede that I am not quite sure what lies ahead, and if you ask me where I want to be in ten years, I can give you a detailed, vivid description, but I would not be the least bit surprised if at thirty-two I am nothing like what I thought I would be at twenty-two. I think those are things worth embracing; worth cherishing; worth laughing and dreaming about. They're instrumental to our development as youth, assisting in the dissipation of our self-subscribed silver spoons and teaching us the essentials of hard work, love, and sacrifice. That's what emotional maturity is, and though I won't give Trina credit for bringing about that realization, she certainly forced me to evaluate these truths in a more holistic context. For that, I am eternally grateful.

Chapter 6

Life: Pain and Porn

Do you not know that your bodies are members of Christ himself? Shall I then take the members of Christ and unite them with a prostitute? Never! Do you not know that he who unites himself with a prostitute is one with her in body? For it is said, "The two will become one flesh." But whoever is united with the Lord is one with him in spirit.

Flee from sexual immorality. All other sins a person commits are outside the body, but whoever sins sexually, sins against their own body. Do you not know that your bodies are temples of the Holy Spirit, who is in you, whom you have received from God? You are not your own; you were bought at a price. Therefore honor God with your bodies. (I Corinthians 15:15–20 NLT)

It's two o'clock in the morning. I'm dripping sweat, partly because of the anxiety I have allowed to build up in my mind, and partly from the overwhelming war being waged inside of me. I've been asleep for hours. Simply falling asleep was an accomplishment—a feat to be both proud and skeptical of. I thought I'd won the battle, but I had only been able to lay claim to victory temporarily, because this opponent, this beast staring me in the eye for every second of the scheduled twelve rounds, she knows not of being saved by the bell. She is relentless. She doesn't sleep, and she never takes a day off. She's got more consecutive workdays than Cal Ripken and Jamaicans combined, and though she suffers defeat, she keeps her eyes set on the goal at hand. So while I walk, steadily pacing my room, the hallways, the kitchen, and then back to my room, there she is—lying in wait, merely waiting for the opportunity to pounce and go all in. I've learned something of relative importance: this Little Lady doesn't play fair. She has no filter. Did I mention she's relentless? She cares nothing about your well-being and even less about your dignity. She looks to alter your definition and expectations of love, compromise, intimacy, and security. She makes you feel triumphant for a moment and riddles you with shame and insecurities the next. She is ruthless and scornful; hateful and filled with greed. I would flat out tell you her name, but I am comfortable in ascertaining that you know of her already. Most of us do. I used to think it was just me, but when I got older and became a bit more transparent, I found I wasn't the only one in my circle constantly losing every battle against her. Then, for some apparent reason, whether the attractiveness of the topic, the recognition that a profitable market existed, or the actual willingness of the community to address it, it came to my attention that a hefty majority of men within the evangelical circle hadn't cracked the correct cheat code. Finally, as I got deeper into the ministry, people saw and felt enough in me to confide some of their deepest and most intimate secrets. You can probably guess what's coming next. During my time leading Our Daily Bread Ministries at West Georgia, it didn't matter whom I spoke with. If there was an ounce of unadulterated transparency, it was revealed—by both parties, mind you—that this Little Lady seemed to have a stranglehold over both of our lives. For so long, I thought this lady had her opponents ironed out. Like Floyd Mayweather, she knew she was the best, but she still took the time to carefully select her challengers. I was wrong; it wasn't just young men scrambling to assemble the pieces to this seemingly unbreakable puzzle—it was young women as well. So we would pray; and we would talk; and then, we would pray some more. And it would be just me and the person sitting across from me. And we would talk about how we fight, and how some nights are better than others, and how sometimes we find ourselves fighting in the morning even more than at night, and how sometimes, we don't even fight at all, we just give in to our desires. And we would sulk in our despair; take comfort in our conviction; encourage one another; vow to do better. I don't know if all or even most of the people I shared those moments with *actually* did better. I've stayed in touch with some of them, and some have done better, kept fighting. Others, not so much. As much as I would like to classify myself in the first category, there are still so many parts of me that unfortunately possess characteristics not unlike a person in the second.

Dear brethren, I beseech you, by the mercies of God, to offer your bodies as living sacrifice, and to let that be your honorable service, and to make a commitment to that at a young age. Do absolutely everything you can to place filters in the way of your lustful imagination, because if you do not, the road to recovery is a long, painful, lonely path.

It's two thirty in the morning now. A half hour has passed, but the struggle remains the same. I couldn't go back to sleep, so I've turned the television on. It can't stay on ESPN, because I've had too many encounters with the Little Lady while *Sportscenter* played in the background. I flip it from the nightly sports highlights and find an episode of *Home Improvement*. I leave it there, but after forcing myself to chuckle at humor that it takes me four and half seconds to realize is not so humorous, I make my way to the fridge. I grab the orange juice and take it with me back to my room. Though I am unsure of what the day will bring once my 6:50 a.m. alarm goes off, I unequivocally know that the rest of this night will be an extremely unforgiving one. Funny thing is, I could have sworn this battle was over. Not permanently, because as long as my earthly body has breath, it will never be over. This I understand, and this I accept. But for this evening, for these next four or five hours, I thought I had overcome the very thing that always seemed to overcome me.

Now it's two thirty, only this time it's the afternoon. I managed to press the snooze button on my alarm two times without making my hands any bloodier, or stickier, than they already are. I finally made it to bed the night before. I took my buddy Jonathon's advice and, at that moment when my favorite URL or DVD was about to encapsulate my brain, I somehow found the urge to do push-ups instead. When the push-ups got tiring, or it started feeling as if I was doing push-ups as a precursor to my intimate encounter, I'd turn the Xbox on. By now, you know I have a fairly vivid imagination, and I take a loss in the Elite Eight on College Hoops 2K8 just as hard as a loss in real life. You can say what you like, but those tools helped me survive—for the night, anyway. They served their purpose. They were temporary distractions and helped me redirect my heart's evil desire and passion toward something that may not be so glorifying to God but certainly isn't as deadly and sadistic (in moderation, of course). So it would seem my battle was over; it had been won. I could freely laugh and work as the day passed without any physiological swoop of burning sensation seemingly taking over me. You'd be surprised, perhaps even astonished, to know just how short-lived that anticipation is.

Just as the snooze gets slapped for the second time, and simultaneously as my two feet hit the carpet and attempt to arise from the bed, the war is back on. I would like to say those few hours of sleep are a truce; that myself and the enemy agree to some sort of Sunday or holiday agreement, just enough so the both of us have a chance to re-up on supplies and enjoy something distinct, necessary, and beneficial in our view. But this Little Lady, if you don't already know her, that's not how she works. She doesn't take breaks. She doesn't give you rest. She has no respect for your feelings and could give two blueberries about how early you have to be up the next morning. Over the years, as we have tangled with one another more and more, she's started showing me a more sick and seductive side of her. At times, her power seems limitless, like a moth to a flame with gasoline eternally being showered over her. Consciousness was formally a requirement for picking a fight. Now, she attacks while my senses are at their lowest, my alerts less heightened, and my weapons stationary and unclean. This is who she is, and she has no shame about it. She will never apologize and has never forfeited. Her will to win is unmatched.

So now it's three o'clock in the afternoon. And I should mention I made it out of my room and out of the apartment this morning. But you should know this was not an easy morning, and in some ways, the battle was much tougher once the sun came up than when it was down. It was almost like she willfully crept into hiding, permitting me to momentarily rest in the falsity of my not-so-present idols in an effort to establish a killer attack in the morning. This was one of those "good" mornings for me, though. I expected it. I was waiting for it. I knew she hadn't gone anywhere. I knew she was lurking, waiting for the right opportunity to pounce and proclaim victory. So before my fingers lifted a toothbrush or pressed the power button on the tube, I hit my knees. Even in writing that, I feel weakened and ashamed, because I've distorted my view of so many things in so many ways that merely talking about taking a knee is utterly repulsive. That's the depth of my sinful infatuation with her. She's corrupted my mind, and for so many years, I've allowed her to. So I guess it shouldn't come as much of a shock that on a beautiful sixty-two-degree day in the middle of fall, not a cloud in the sky, though I'm surrounded by so many people and have not an ounce of an expectation of privacy, my mind is at war now. It's almost like a Cold War, in the sense that there's no actual warfare. I'm not in a position to search the web, pop a DVD in, or unbuckle my belt. This chess game is taking place in my mind, one second at a time, with nearly every woman I walk past, no matter how clothed she is. It helps, really helps, if she leaves something to the imagination, but most of them have left my imagination to naught today, and here I am, trembling at the sound of the screech of a desk chair or a yawn or a bang of the knee that remotely resembles the noises I etched into my brain in my bed a few nights before. If this were a football game, I'd be losing 17–0 right now. But the bookies and television executives can't really analyze or place a line on this, because I've seen how this ends too many times.

    I fight, or at least I try to pretend to. Some days are better than others. That whole mind game I've just recounted for the last hour and a half—that was while in class. Now the peak of the battle has officially begun. Butterflies begin to flutter away in my stomach, and as the professor finally dismisses class, Sal and Johnny are imaginatively in the corner. Sal bets the next round that I'll fail miserably within an hour. Johnny has a little more faith in me, as he ups the ante to the next two rounds if I fall in the next two hours instead of one. Sadly, both of them have higher expectations than I do for myself—never mind that I have a meeting with my professor shortly after class. No, that kind of stuff matters not. When she calls your name, you answer. Of course you don't want to answer, because you know it'll be better if you press the ignore button, or even if you flirt with the idea of acknowledging the call but find the will to let it go to voice mail. But that's how it feels. She calls so often. She never gets the picture, because to her, there is no picture. She's spoiled, and she will have what and who she wants when she wants. Sometimes, she intentionally leaves a voice mail, because she likes to plant seeds. She knows you may not pickup for the conversation now, but if she can whisper a sweet nothing in your ear that she can bring back to your remembrance hours later when you are all alone, she knows her win probability increases substantially.

I wish it mattered that a meeting was scheduled, or that Bible study at church was merely hours away, or that I had so intimately experienced God just a few nights ago. All those things *should* matter, but in reality, when the bell rings, she makes all those meaningful encounters temporarily disappear. She changes the way you think and removes your sensible ability. The meeting is important, but it can always be rescheduled. My recently scheduled appointment with *her* is of the utmost importance, and though she will always be lying at the door, I feel nothing matters in life right now more than me opening it.

After all this time—the fighting, pain, discomfort, and embarrassment—and all we've been through internally in just the past sixteen hours, all the images created, removed, reopened, and cast down and the mental energy expended trying to break my mind and heart loose from the chains of her, she wins. I give in. I gave up. I failed. Back to square one. God is displeased with me. This is how I feel at least.

The Porn Monster: Clarity

Let's clarify a few things. Sin is sin. Period. There is no justification for it, and God is not pleased with it. It stings and should convict; it litters the sweet aroma of the presence of God with stench and filth. It hinders our ability to hear from and form a fellowship with God. In our minds, it can tarnish the power of His Word and Spirit. So be it with the Monster. It is not OK to indulge her. What you are about to read is merely a portion of my life's testimony and why she has been such a weight in my life for so long. In essence, it is an account and explanation of why I have chosen to self-medicate with her for so many years. Accounts and explanations, however, are not justifications. They do not change the fact that I have committed this sin before God countless times over. Thankfully, He is not like man. Heck, I don't even feel right saying He, as God is genderless; He's not a human being, so He's not confined to our relational standards or reasoning. (But that's a totally different topic.)

I visit a lot of blogs and discuss this issue with a lot of people. It has become one of my favorite topics, because so many people are struggling with it. Throughout my conversations, I have noted that some women feel as if the issue of the Monster has progressed to the point of sensitivity and borderline acceptance. Granted, most women understand that this is not intentionally the message, but with the science associated with the Monster increasingly showing that there are serious neurological implications associated with pornography addiction some are beginning to feel as if the level of accountability and expectation for men, and even some women, struggling to win their war against the Monster is being lessened. There's the proverbial "I'm a man; I'm going to struggle with this. I can't help it" tension coming from a faction of the church. If this is you, as it has been me at times, we need to repent.

Men, think about the example we set for our sons and daughters and the pain we put our wives through as a result of pornography. How alone and undesirable do our women feel when their husbands would rather watch a video than lay with them? I am not an expert on women. I don't think anyone truly is. (If someone were, that person would be richer than Bill Gates.) What I do know, unequivocally, is that women, when they trust you to the point that they will marry, move in with, share finances, and share a bed with you, they love you. They will do virtually anything for you and to please you. They will do things they've spent decades saying they will never do for any man lovingly, sacrificially, and sexually. Men, those are pleasures that we must earn in constant pursuit of our bride. She wants to be provided for and protected, but she also wants you to desire her. She wants to be sexual and vulnerable with you. As she ages and her once-flat stomach adds weight and firm breasts start sagging, she wants to know that you find her as stunning now as you did years before. How would you feel if you spent your life faithful to your wife, denying yourself the opportunity to share sexual experiences with anyone other than her, only to find out that she'd rather touch herself while standing in a computer chair than make love to us?

Let me be abundantly clear as a single, twenty-two-year-old man who saw his first pornographic image at the age of eleven and who is arguably in the peak sexual years of his life: there is absolutely no justification for a life of unrepented sin. Period. If you are a porn addict, go get help. If you like ordering porn through your cable service, cut off the cable. If you can't stop watching porn on your smart phone, get rid of it. This is more directed at men than at women, so excuse me if the tone seems a bit harsh, but it is time for men to be men in this area of their lives.

Men love to say they're men when it's convenient. We love watching sports and drinking beer and reminding our wives that we are the leaders of our households, yet we can't control our minds long enough to let the Holy Spirit remind us that the eight seconds of pleasure that comes with pornography leads to shame, regret, remorse, and eventually death—of both body and mind. I don't say this as someone who never falls into the pornographic trap anymore. I do say this as someone who has found strength in Christ Jesus and has gone through many stretches of clean living that I know would not have happened without the work of the Holy Spirit. I want that cleanliness to be who I am permanently, but it will take time. I didn't turn my mind into a landfill overnight, so I acknowledge that I must triple my efforts to dispose of her. That's what it takes, men. We'll discuss in-depth approaches, both practically and spiritually, that will help you win the war against the Monster. For now, you must commit to the fight. That means being a man and throwing away the magazine you keep under the bed "just in case." It means deleting the naked photographs of your girlfriend from your external hard drive. It means not entertaining the conversation of anyone who will put your mind in a compromising position that ends in a pornographic image or sound. This is all-out war, gentlemen. Your senses must always be on and your weapons at your disposal. Your guard must always be on full alert. This is a struggle, not an acceptance. By the grace, power, and spirit of the Lord, you will overcome it. Fight.

The Porn Monster: Evolution

I was with my cousin Jason one summer day in the early 2000s. We were at my grandfather's house eagerly awaiting dinner. I was in the back room directly adjacent to the bathroom when he got there. It was my aunt's room, which could have been a contestant on the "Who can stuff the most stuff into one room?" show, if such a show existed. I was in the back, flipping through channels, and I had settled on one of the more popular music video channels, which churned out Backstreet Boys and N'Sync at record paces all day. (I loved both of those groups, by the way. Judge!) Jason knocked on the door and, without waiting for a response, tiptoed into the room. I didn't mind. I was slightly lonely because I had been around females virtually all day, so it was nice to have some testosterone enter the building. For some reason, I felt compelled to start flipping through the channels again. I suppose it was something from one of the music videos that triggered something in me. Whatever it was, in retrospect, it didn't end very well. By now you have likely realized that this particular story doesn't end well. I thought about going into the details of it, but I realized that it's probably just too much information. But know this: I did not fall into the snaring trap of pornography by choice. Our society—this oversexed culture we live in—slowly but surely lured me in. Trust me, I am one of the biggest proponents of personal responsibility. I do not blame anyone else for my sin except myself. Nonetheless, when you're a child and you start to experience hormones that are meant for men but you don't yet have the self-control or submission of a man, it can be tough to cope. Once you add in the fact that nearly *everything* in America is sold by using sex, it's tough to battle the forces of the world as child.

In a nutshell, this afternoon with Jason, well, as I said, it didn't end well. I had seen suggestive music videos and images from magazines, but as we were aimlessly flipping channels on the cable box, I saw my first pornographic image. It wasn't intentional, and I surely had not sought it out. Regardless of how we got there, however, I felt like Pandora's box had been opened in such a massive way. I think that's one of the many problems with the Monster.

A Memoir: On Love and Life

Once I got exposed to her, I became more and more curious. At twelve years old, you're already curious, and compiling images and videos on top of that curiosity only drives your desire to further kill the cat. (No pun intended.) I realize a lot of things in retrospect. (Yes, life is always seen best through the lens of hindsight.) One of the ways the Monster aims to kill your soul and your intimacy is not only the literal availability of it, but also the wide range of availability. For example, if you want to, you can go on the Internet right now, free of charge, and fantasize about nearly any person of any body type doing any number of things for any amount of time. Now, think about an entire generation of youth (not just boys) who have that expectation of sexuality as they become adults, because they have been so accustomed to feeding that desire all throughout adolescence. That's scary. (To say the least.)

No, I am not arguing that the Monster lends herself to creating a society where young men demand outlandish things of women sexually, and if they aren't satisfied, they resort to violent or hurtful means of getting it (though I would not entirely rule that out as a potential consequence). Instead, it becomes frightening to our societal views and expectations of monogamy and sexuality. This is a place where faith and mere morality intersect. Even if I were an atheist, I would not want my son growing up and being able to satisfy *any* of his sexual fantasizes or desires with three clicks of the mouse, because that expectation, even if it doesn't turn into violence or addiction, is dangerous for his mental, psychological, and emotional health. I don't want him to grow up thinking women are a weaker sex (because they are not) or that they are mostly just objects of sexual gratification for men (because they are not). Subconsciously, whether one wants to admit it or not, that's one of the consequences of a generation raised on pornography just as much as they were raised on *Harry Potter* and *Hannah Montana*. Even if you *say* you don't devalue the preciousness of sexuality, intimacy, and the opposite sex, desensitization can only be held off for so long. At some point, those images start to etch themselves into your everyday evaluation of first-person experiences. Thus, when you interact with a member of the opposite sex or see one walking by, your immediate reaction is to tell your friends how you would "hit that" or "he can get it." It's

A Memoir: On Love and Life

not an expectation that sexuality will no longer be a part of our everyday conversations, but there should be an expectation that sexuality will no longer be *the* focal point of our conversations.

What does this mean? It means that men who call themselves Christians can finally have conversations where women are referenced without talking about "how bad she is." It means women can stop talking about how much they need to get married because "they have needs." Now, don't get me wrong: I love women. I admire their beauty in more ways than one. I love the Creator, but to be perfectly honest with you, I am not oblivious to the beauty of his creations. Even so, there's a point of admiration and appreciation that does not tilt into the realm of lust.[5]

In essence, my bout with the Monster is a direct result of my sin, but it's not just the sin of actually putting in a DVD or clicking the mouse more times than I should. It's about allowing God to change my mind all times of the day, in all situations, and concerning all circumstances. When I partake in certain unfruitful

---

[5] Mind you, right now, I am talking about this from the prospective of a single person. I believe the rules for "admiration of members of the opposite sex" change a bit once you take vows, but I'll be able to discuss that more in the coming years (or at least I hope so).

conversations, it's like taking three steps backward when I've taken one step ahead. Participating in conversations centered on sexuality can be just as damaging as actually watching a video. It's akin to cruel and unusual punishment. You've got this thing, this person who is ready to move on to the next life, but you keep taking it on and off life support. You say you've buried the old you who used to run home to surf the web for lewd videos and images. If that person is really gone, stop visiting that gravesite with a shovel known as lewd conversations. You may not be able to change the fact that you were exposed to this sin or the fact that you developed a habit for pornography before knowing it was a sin, but you can control how much you allow yourself to feed this ungodly desire. It's a blazing forest fire, and though it may potentially take you years to completely control it, don't willfully bring matches to the center of the blaze. Focus your energy on putting it out.

A Fine Line: Addiction or Submission?

My struggles have been well documented, partly because I am intentional about documenting them myself. Nonetheless, as I get older, mature in my faith, and slowly but surely learn what it means to *really* fight sin, a burning question begins to turn in my head: where's the line between pornography addition and blatant inability to submit to the will of God? I feel like I am qualified to answer this question. After all, I have struggled with this for *years*, and though I learned ways to tame it, mostly through the Holy Spirit and some thorough, practical steps, there seems to be more that needs to be explored.

Of late, more and more people in evangelical circles are acknowledging porn addition as an actual addiction. Science has began to prove that repeated exposure to pornography drills itself into the brain, and the chemicals the brain secretes when one is snorting cocaine are the same chemicals a person viewing pornography has ringing through their brain. This shouldn't come as any surprise. God made us all sexual creatures, and I believe He designed sex to have a mesmerizing effect on us. This is why He intended for it to be used within marriage with one person of the opposite sex. Any other use or view of sexuality is outside of God's designed plan. This includes pornography, and even pornographic images and videos that try to advertise themselves as being intimate, romantic, or sensual.

Since we know the true meaning and purpose of sex, and we are well aware that nearly all of us, in some capacity, have not honored its sacredness, it's time to do a little soul-searching. To be blunt, I used to think I was a "porn addict." After all, I would indulge in it multiple times per day, and no matter how hard I tried, when my mind went there, it stayed there until I fed its perverted desires. Over the years, however, through prayer, scripture reading, and a greater appreciation and emotional connection to sports, writing, and video games, my pursuit of said sin has dwindled. Nonetheless, I finally realized that I wasn't a porn addict during a trip overseas. My phone didn't work, I didn't bring my computer, there was no Internet at any of the hotels I stayed in, and my time there (I was studying abroad in Western Europe) had been scheduled down to the minute; I simply didn't have the ability to watch pornography. That was an eighteen-day trip. *Eighteen* days. At the time, whenever I would get puffed up and want to brag about how many days I had gone without indulging in it, I would look at a calendar and notice that what felt like seven or eight days had only really been two or three days without it. I got back home from that trip and was confronted with so many conflicting emotions spiritually. I then had to ask myself, "How much is this pornography thing more about increasing my ability to submit to the will of God than it is addiction?"

Let's get one thing straight: there are men and women out there who are honestly addicted to pornography, and those men and women need both prayer and professional assistance. I am not degrading or belittling their struggle. They need the support of their Christian brothers and sisters as they acknowledge their failings and shortcomings and strive to make much of Christ in their sexuality. On the flip side, I know many men and women (mostly men) who are *not* addicts. Instead, we sit around the house for a few days, or have a long day at work or school, and are tempted by the slightest image or noise and fail to equip ourselves with the tools necessary to choose the promises of Christ over the temporal allure of sin. Don't worry, you don't have to admit it; I'll be the example for you.

After my European trip, I had gone eighteen days without viewing, seeing, or indulging in any kind of pornography. It wasn't like I was in Mongolia or Chad. I was in first-world, developed, sex-crazed Western nations, where, if I had *really* wanted to, I could have picked up a magazine or video for a few Euros and no one would have thought much of it. At that moment, I asked myself, "Can cocaine addicts, unless they're recovering, go eighteen days without cocaine? Do alcoholics go eighteen days without a drink? Do sex addicts go eighteen days without being compelled to visit the closest red-light district?"

For me, labeling my lustful struggles as an addiction had become a scapegoat. In many ways, it made it easier to pick myself up after a shameful deed. Calling it an addiction, instead of calling it what it was, sin, made me feel better about myself. I was less ashamed of what I had just chosen to do, but it diminished my view of God's majesty. Over and over, I succumbed to temptation, and in the back of my mind, I justified it by calling it an addiction.

I have since learned that, though lust is one of the larger struggles in my life, I am far from a porn addict. Instead, in the words of Felix Moten[6], sin is always lying at the door. The opportunity to give into that which is deceitful will present itself repeatedly as long as we occupy these present bodies with these carnal minds. We have to become more intentional about fighting those temptations and not letting the temporary pleasure of sin cloud our view of the awesome and eternal king. So how do we do that? I'm glad you asked.

Fight

I suppose that each person who struggles with lust has different strategies and tactics that work well for him or her. Personally, I have found John Piper's ANTHEM to be effective sometimes. (Use your favorite online search engine and look it up.) Though I am normally not a fan of steps and checklists, I found this method to be tremendously useful when fighting battles like these. In a moment's notice, you need to easily remind yourself of what needs to be done to stay in the will of God, and

---

[6] Felix Moten is Pastor of Word of Truth Christian Church in Bremen, Georgia.

numbered steps might help you do that better than a series of long paragraphs.

1. Be Relational

With God. That's where it starts. We aim to please Him; to make much of Him; to glorify Him; to radiate His goodness and His awesomeness. We do not refrain from pornography, or any other sexual act outside of marriage, to bring ourselves great pride or accomplishment. Instead, we submit our sexual desires to His will. That said, for a temptation that often seems so incredibly strong, it's going to be absurdly difficult to bypass not doing something for someone if you never spend time with that person. If I'm not reading, praying, and fasting, I can't expect that I am going to be able to fight temptation, because I'm not spending time with the one who gives me strength to fight. Sermons on sexual purity are nice. Books on theology serve their purpose in the fight. At the end of the day, however, we must indulge in the Lord. We have to find power and strength in His Word and through our prayer lives, and we must cling to it.

A Memoir: On Love and Life

Say you become a parent one day. In this example, we'll use a male. When I become a father, I want my children to know that I love and adore them. I want them to know that there is nothing in this world I won't do for them. I want to be there for them through everything life brings about. I could not imagine the level of hurt and emptiness I would feel if my twelve-year-old only wanted to hang out with me for food or sports tickets. I'd be devastated if the extent of our relationship was him coming to me only when he was struggling with his math homework. I want to be there through the ups and downs, experiencing every little nuance of life and love. Yet I can't help but think this is how we make God feel so often. Not only do we turn God into a genie, we only come to Him after we make a mistake, or when we need or want something done that will enable us to feel better about ourselves. That's not a relationship. It's more of a business model, and it's a bad business model at that. God wants us to overcome this struggle because He wants us to experience sex the way it *should be* experienced: within the confines of marriage; with one person; in a monogamous relationship. Yes, there's grace for those of us who have shifted away from this design, but getting back on track and encountering the joy of its true design starts with an understanding, appreciation, and relationship with the Creator. Read. Pray. Fast. Love.

2. Get Rid of It

Every pornographic anything you have anywhere near you—get rid of it. Light and darkness cannot coexist (1 John 1:6). Delete all of it off of your computer and external hard drive. Place an accountability filter on your phone. Downgrade your cable television package. If you can't stop watching porn on your smartphone, get rid of it. Period. I say these things as person who, at some point, has had to undertake these steps myself.

A few months after getting a brand-new Windows phone, one that allowed me to write papers, journal entries, and short stories on it, I gave it away to a friend in exchange for a small, ho-hum Nokia phone. I told her I wanted to switch because I preferred a phone with a keyboard. I didn't lie; I just told a partial truth. After weeks of searching for an accountability and/or filter software for the phone, I decided I couldn't handle it. I was not strong enough to have a phone that gave me access to the Monster anywhere at any time with the simple click of two buttons. Thus, the smartphone, for which I had paid roughly $260, had to go. The wages of sin is death. In the grand scheme of things, it was a fairly easy decision.

On top of that, I went the last two years of my undergraduate career without a computer. As a law student, I am still not sure how I managed that. All of my work for class had to be done in my office or at the library, which meant an inordinate amount of nights and weekends were spent outside of the comfort of my apartment. I couldn't handle having a computer. It may be sad, but it's so incredibly true. This is the fervency with which we have to fight sin. Are the video games you play on your PS4 worth you being able to view pornography at the flick of your joystick?

3. Replace It

When that feeling of temptation comes over you, there has to be something you can fix your mind on in addition to Jesus—something that can help you overcome the moment. I used to believe that needing to replace my fleshly desire to indulge in pornography was a concession that Christ was not enough to overcome. In all actuality, it's quite the opposite. It's a total surrender of the faith you have in yourself. Remember when Jesus told Peter that, before the rooster crowed, he would deny him three times? Peter emphatically stated that he would never forsake the Christ.[7] Well, I think the sin of greatest measure, the one we can learn most from, is not the actual moment when Peter said, "I've never seen this man before." Instead, the most impactful sin happened at the table, when Peter told Jesus he would not deny him. In that moment, Peter placed his faith in his own ability, rather than placing it in the hands of the Spirit. He thought that because of his relationship with Jesus and seeing Him do these miraculous things, he would instantly revert to a willingness to die alongside the Savior of the world. That just wasn't the case. I used to think about my lustful temptations in a similar vein. Relationship and isolation can be helpful steps to winning the war. As a matter of fact, relationship and periodic exclusion are key steps to overcoming the battle, but you have to

---

[7] We know how that ended—Peter denied Christ two times before Jesus made it to the cross. (John 13:36–38 and Matthew 26:69–74)

recognize that you, in your fleshly state, may not be able to overcome this simply by virtue of reading your bible and getting rid of your smartphone. If you're *really* an addict, or even someone who is just massively struggling, you'll find creative ways to get access to it, even if you cut off your Internet, buy a flip phone, and burn all of your DVDs. Additionally, you also must take into account the depth of the sin going on in your mind. The actual click of the mouse or press of the play button is merely a manifestation of the heart's deceitfulness. By the time the image uploads or the video starts, you have already sinned against the Lord in your mind. At this point, everything else that takes place is merely, for lack of a better reference, icing on the cake. Thus, it is imperative to change your mind. Yes, I know that changing your mind is much easier said than done, which is why you must replace your lustful thoughts with passion or exuberance for something else, and you must do it as soon as the thought creeps into your head.

  In undergrad, I played *a lot* of video games. It got to the point that I would take my franchises in various sports video games *too* seriously. For a quick second, I thought the level of passion I was putting into video games was a bit too much, but it dawned on me that the time I had formerly spent surfing the net for soul-killing images was now being used to figure out how to stop LeBron James in the NBA finals. It wasn't the most beneficial replacement, but if you ask me to choose between video games and a habit that, if left unchecked and unrepentant, leads to hell, there's not much of a choice there.

Video games might not be your thing. Regardless, you do have a *thing*. There's a room that needs to be cleaned. Your grandmother needs stuff done around the house. Your roommate needs help fixing his car. There's laundry to get done. There are weights to be lifted. You have female friends who need their trash taken out or oil changed. Go do something! Find something to take your mind off the passions of the flesh, and make that your everything for as long as it takes for the promises of God to win out over the temporary pleasure of Satan.

Hope for Those in Battle

I know all too well how horrendous it feels to fall over and over again. The stint of sin and sting of conviction remains the same. In fact, over time, it doesn't even become an enjoyable sin, because it takes merely seconds for you to drop your head in shame. You've made vow after vow and said prayer after prayer, and yet it seems you make no progress in this particular area of your spiritual life. The first thing you should do in the hours after these moments of despair is thank God. I know it sounds weird, and it is completely contrary to everything you have just partaken in, but conviction is a sign that the Holy Spirit lives inside of you, and the Holy Spirit living inside of you means you have repented of your sins, and you repenting of your sins means that the sting and penalty of *all* of your sins has been conquered by Jesus on the cross and through his resurrection. When it becomes hard to find joy in the midst of what seems like perpetual failure, find solace in the fact that your sins have already been forgiven.

You may employ nearly every practical step possible, and yet, sin may fall before you. It happens. That's a natural consequence of living in this world and residing in a mortal body. Nonetheless, I implore you, brothers and sisters, do not quit. Keep fighting. Every time you succumb to temptation, get up off the mat and dedicate yourself to an even tougher fight next time around. It hurts. You feel like you've constantly let God down and that you don't deserve His love, grace, or mercy. In all actuality, we *don't* deserve it. That's the great thing. All of our sin, not just our sexual sin, separates us from God. As a result of it, we should be in the land of dead, weeping and gnashing our teeth in the absence of our Creator. But the amazing thing about God is that He loved us so much that while we were still sinners—still fornicating, lying, cheating, masturbating, and being sharp with our tongues,[8]—He loved us so much that he sent his son to die for us (Romans 5:8). So let *that* be the only encouragement you need for your next battle. Do whatever it takes to continue to pick yourself up off the pavement. If your heart is pure and you have a genuine desire to please God in your personal life, He will continue to work on you, and you will find deliverance in His perfect and ordained time.

Sexuality

Sex and sensuality are, without question, my favorite topics, but not for obvious reasons. We are all sexual beings.

---

[8] Along with a litany of other things

There's a part of all of us that yearns to have passionate, vulnerable, intimate sex on a Saturday in February while the heavens drop an inch of rain. Lately, my fascination with sexuality has catapulted to levels I am not even sure I understand.

For a long time, in my mind, sex was merely about the physical act of intercourse, and my thoughts, pursuits, and passions didn't go any further than that. There was little thought or concern given to why I should wait to do this until I get married or how it would affect my ability to be in relation with Christ and discern His voice from my own desires and temptations. So let's just get a few things straight:

1. I've made my fair share of mistakes.

I know. It sucks. *Really.* I don't believe in having regrets. There's no huge philosophical view of it. Life is too short to spend any amount of time wishing you had done something differently, because the fact of the matter is, you can't go back and change anything. You can learn from those mistakes and vow to be different and better going forward, but you can't change the past. With that said, if there were anything I would want to change about my life, it wouldn't be any of the various trials or tribulations I've discussed in this book. Instead, I would abstain from intercourse until marriage. (Even that has its talking points, but we'll get to that in a second.) I am focusing on the fact that I am not a virgin not to shed light on my ability to sleep with women (a. because it's not really an ability; b. because it's sin; c. because that would just be awkward). I say that to illustrate to everyone in their teenage to young adult years that I know how you feel, literally. I know what it's like to stare temptation in the face, to feel things in your body, mind, heart, and soul that you've never felt before and yet not be able to act on those desires. It's natural, and though it comes with a high degree of difficulty, it's imperative that you continue to submit those feelings to the will of God.

2. Sex is meant for marriage.

Period. I will not discuss this further. That's as simple as it gets. Sex should be explored with your spouse after, and only after, you have taken a vow before God and His people to establish a covenant between you two that will last until you perish. Now, I say God *and* His people because I so often hear excuses like "well, we're going to get married" or "we're pretty much a married couple." I am not a fan of playing house. We have weddings, however big or small, so that our friends, family, and closest confidants can be witnesses to the vows we take before each other. In many ways, it is a source of accountability and recognition. This is my lawfully wedded, whom I promise to love, honor, cherish, and adore, and if I my actions ever seem to run counterintuitive to that (as they are most certainly prone to at some point in the marriage) you may lovingly point me back on track. One of my favorite things to see in public is a couple in love. It's so encouraging and flattering. I used to not like holding hands or kissing in public, or sharing in any kind of public displays of affection. I don't see my attitude about PDA changing all that much in the future, but I do look forward to gripping my wife's hand as we stroll through the city from time to time, or stealing a kiss from her lips while she's in midsentence. You want a partner who is into you and who doesn't mind telling the world that they are into you. Before you physically let someone inside of you or go inside of someone else, that person ought have the courage, decency, and love to tell the world he or she adores you and will gladly forsake all others in devotion to you. It's not a money issue. I've seen small weddings. I know couples comprised of two people still in school who have gotten creative in their wedding and honeymoon planning. I understand wanting to give a young lady her dream wedding or honeymoon before getting married, but she (or he) must also understand that, if you really love each other, those things will come in due time. In the interim, if you are not ready to marry, you are not ready for sex. Do not negotiate that premise with anyone.

3. **Pornography is not sex.**

Libraries of false images are etched into the brains of many of us. From a young age, what we see on television or in magazines or on computer screens is what we see as sexuality. That's just not the case. Porn does an array of damage, but perhaps the most severe damage it does is hinder our expectations of sexuality. You don't watch an action movie and believe you can jump off buildings and fight eleven people with guns at the same time and still be alive to go home with the hot Russian woman at the bar, do you?[9] The same thing applies to pornography. Those men and women are actors, and the horrors they experience before and after the scenes are done playing are rarely shared. Our views and expectations of sexuality should not come from videos; they should be conformed to the will of God, and our expression and expectations of sexuality should be limited to the desires of our spouses. As a male, if your sexual expectations are based on what you see in pornographic films, you will be woefully displeased with your wife. No, that is not your spouse's problem. She does not need to become more of a "freak" or open herself up to more things in order to make you happy. Instead, it is your job to pray to God and ask him to cleanse your impure heart, mind, and soul. It is your job to love your wife to the fullest, making her every need and desire yours, so as to ensure that the feeling of intimacy you share with her in the marriage bed is an extension of the intimacy you share throughout the day. Porn wraps your mind in fantasy worlds, creating disillusions of pleasure. In an effort to free my mind from the impurity of pornography, I ask God to create in me a clean heart. I know my sin has ravaged my purity,

---

[9] This is not a rhetorical question. The answer is NO!

and when the time does come to be intimate with my wife, I want to be totally lost in her; in her desires and her pleasures; in what she longs for and enjoys. Pornography clouds that experience; it makes it more difficult to experience true ecstasy with your lawfully wedded spouse. Porn is not sex. Porn is deceitful. Do not let it define your expectations of sexuality.

4. Like, I *really* love sex.

But what is it about sexuality that makes it such a compelling subject? As I got older, I realized I loved the nuances of sex, the noises and vulnerability, the sweat, and the nails pinched into my back just as much, if not more, than the actual act. I took note of the fact that I loved yellow nail polish on lighter-skinned women and white on those with darker complexions, and that accents, scents, and asking me questions about my little brother did more for me than breast size. I understand why I felt these things, and though I'll refrain from sharing, it made me ponder my sexuality more.

When it comes to sex in the church, the lone message to singles seems to be: "Don't have it. Deny yourself. Stay away from it." That's cool. I totally understand that premise; after all, Paul said to flee fornication for a reason. There are moments of temptation where dialogue and psychological exploration need to cease in favor of the superior wisdom and power of the Holy Spirit. But for me, a guy who loves the nuances of the opposite sex and longs to merely be able to love a woman, I found there were times when talking about it actually helped me through my temptation.

What I noticed, throughout interactions with many other singles, and after dissecting my own view of marriage and sexuality, which had developed through years of church attendance, is that I had placed sex on this incomprehensible pedestal. In many ways, I had made sex within an institution that I wasn't even close to entering an idol. Every time I would see a beautiful woman on television or hear anything related to sex, I automatically reverted to the thought process of, "I can't wait to get married"—as if taking vows would ease the depths of my lust. There's a place for that. Trust me, I can't wait to get married and have sex, but I have learned to guard against making an idol of it. I realized that the idol I had made of sex within marriage was no better than the idol I had made of sex and sexual images outside of marriage. Both were blatant sin. My pursuit of purity had begun to be something I succeeded at when I thought long and hard about my future wife, but pornography and fornication never ceased to be beautifully appealing when I "just" thought about being pure for God. I had everything about sex backward.

What happens if my wife has more female problems than other women and her menstrual cycle is heavier and longer than most, thus decreasing her desire to have sex and her ability to lose herself in it? What if my wife has been abused and doesn't get aroused in conventional ways? Will our marriage suffer because it literally takes an entire day of good deeds and sweet nothings to get her mind at a place where she can lay with me without the demons of her past interfering in our intimacy? What if your wife is thirty years old and is a virgin, and you've created all these dreams of what your first night together will be like, only to realize that she probably won't enjoy sex for a couple of months? There are so many things about our spouses that we do not know, and even more we won't know when it becomes legal for us to be intimate. Sex, done right, is not about your desires, but rather about those of your spouse. A natural man concerns himself with being a stallion. A spiritual man finds pleasure in his wife's pleasure. Do not create images or false expectations of sexuality within marriage, because each of our marriage beds will differ in their experiences, and that so heavily depends on the past emotions, mind, and physical health of another person that you cannot control. Moreover, some of us may find that our marriage beds do not become titillating and exciting without a little bit of work, a load of vulnerability, and a steep serving of patience. This is another falsity some people in the church have fed us millennials throughout our childhood as well—that as long as you wait until you get married, sex will be wonderful, intimate, passionate, and exhilarating from the very beginning with little to no work. Puh-lease! Such a belief inherently stems from a culture wreaking of abstinence-only teaching and not realistic expectations or conversations. Of course, that does not mean that I don't see God as sovereign and sex as something that is meant for married people. However, I am saying that, though we prayerfully hope our sons and daughters wait until their wedding nights to become sexually active, we will do our best to also articulate that there's just as much grace for fornication at fifteen as there is for pornography at twenty-five. This has to be especially true for our daughters, who are consistently drilled with a message that makes it seem like they are nothing more than leftovers if they happen to not make it to their wedding night with their virginity intact. In a lot of ways, this is deplorable—mostly because we don't teach our boys the same thing.

A few pages back, I hinted at a few practical steps that have helped me fight my sexual impulses. Still, I think there's a redemptive quality to indulging in something of a sensual nature to help you through your deepest moments. (Hear me out.) One of my frustrations with some in the church is the idea that, if you simply pray, fast, read your Bible, and ignore or replace your sexual desires momentarily, such a strategy is a winning one that will take you to your wedding night sex, porn, and masturbation free. Without going into detail, I'll simply let you know that I tried that—and it sure as heck didn't work. Lots of things are good. Even more things are necessities. Your body needs them. You fast from food, but at some point, your body demands that you eat something. You can give up water for a little while, but sooner rather than later, you're going to collapse if you're not properly hydrated. In the church, we acknowledge that we need fellowship, which inherently means the company of other people and their physical embrace, but we always tell singles, particularly young ones, to simply wait. Who decided this was a good strategy?

Again, waiting is the ultimate answer. Though you may be frustrated in your wait, it is still that which is biblical and that which is for your own protection. (STDs anyone? Teen pregnancy?) However, one of the biggest aspects of appropriately addressing your sexuality while not actually being able to, you know, have sex, is finding something to replace it. And that doesn't always mean replacing your sexual desires with video games or a phone conversation with your girlfriends, because I believe that can be just as unhealthy. If you spend a decade associating the rising of your hormones with a subsequent urge for *Kingdom Hearts* or dialing your best friend's number, you shouldn't be that surprised when you're not quite able to let go of the shackles and free yourself on your wedding night. So one of the other unconventional ways I used to address my sensuality without covering it with sin was allowing myself to think, talk, and listen about it. Writing this chapter helped me address my sensuality. Reading Song of Songs from time to time helps me address my sensuality. Listening to Keri Hilson's *Make Love* helps me address, and then subsequently subdue, my sensuality. Some people would disagree with these methods, and I respect their right to part ways with my unconventional thinking. Nonetheless, I think simply teaching ourselves to outright ignore our sexuality and sensuality for years, and expecting to magically be able to love and embrace at the drop of a minister's word, is foolish at best. Now, if Beyoncé's *Dance for You* makes me want to spend the night at someone's house after every listen, then yes, I have a problem. However, if I can listen to such songs and use them as channels to address what is, after all, a huge part of who I am, at a phase of life where it's natural to ponder my sexuality with fervency, I think that's a creative, fruitful step to purity that doesn't compromise my sexual desires upon saying "I do."

Recap

I can write an entire book on this subject. (In fact, I think I will!) In the interim, be reminded that our pursuit of purity is not an effort to please our future spouse, it is a pursuit aimed at pleasing our God. Keep things in perspective. What we ignorantly believe are our physical needs now will differ when God brings us together with someone. God knows your physical needs. He gave them to you. He created them with that in mind. Thus, He will meet your physical needs within the context of marriage when the time comes. We trust Him with our finances, schooling, families, health, and salvation; surely we can trust Him with our sex organs, too.

Chapter 7

Life: INsecurity

Life can be cruel, but a lot of the time, the people near you can make it even crueler. It's as if a lot of people base their entire existence on regurgitating useless information that speaks nothing to a person's morals or character. They can be in a room full of people, all of whom seem to be having a festive and fulfilling time, and still have a heart colder than Rose at the end of *Titanic*. For these people, I'm not sure what life is about. I couldn't tell you what the importance of life is to them or what their purpose is. I'm not even sure they could tell you what kind of legacy they want to leave behind on this earth or how they plan on changing the world…or even what drives them to spend so many of their limited hours here assessing and categorizing other people based on their asinine opinions.

I suppose this is probably a maturity thing. After all, I am far from innocent of *ever* passing judgment on people. Truth be told, that last paragraph was probably 67 percent truth, 21 percent judgmental, and 12 percent just how I was feeling at the particular time I wrote this. So bear with me, and if you pray, pray for me. Because, if you've gotten this far, you clearly know and understand just how much of a sinner I am. And my continued prayer is that, through the progression of my sanctification, and as you read this book, and as I continue to grow in my relationships with Christ and His people, that acknowledgment will become more of source of inspiration and adoration toward the Gospel, rather than a copout for failing to meet the example of Jesus. This is a start, I suppose.

I wasn't always so willing or able to accept my mistakes, sins, and faults. To be honest, those recognitions still come with their fair share of stubbornness at the most inopportune times. But life has a way of growing you up and making you a more well-rounded and empathetic individual; even when people around you seem to be set on reminding you of all of the little things you *don't* have.

I was called so many things growing up that if I decided to list all of them it could take up an entire chapter. I'll skip that. Of the many talents, blessings, and natural gifts God gave me, height was not one of them. Through no fault of my own, I ended up being born to a mother who doesn't scratch five feet and a father who isn't exactly Kevin Durant. My entire adolescence was spent playing defense because of this. Given how angry I got sometimes, you would think it was my fault—that I woke up a few mornings and didn't take the garbage out and made a spectacularly stupid bet that led me to be this height…that, contrary to all logic, success and desirability would increase with every increased inch of height. I never fully bought into these things, but I'd be lying if I told you that they *never* affected me; that they *never* kept me up at night; that it *wasn't* one of the key reasons I was so angry growing up.

It always seemed like treading water in enemy territory. My sisters, who are slightly shorter than me, never seemed to have the same problems I did. I suppose the lewdness and vulgarity of others was somewhat tamed because of their gender. After all, if you're female, you're "supposed" to be shorter than your male counterparts, and if you are, it's no big deal. I always felt the opposite, like the world was out to attack and tempt and destroy me simply because I wasn't six foot two. At age eleven, it's a tremendously tough pill to swallow, and when people continuously remind you of your literal shortcoming every day for eight hours a day, five days a week, it makes you literally want to swallow pills…and never wake up.

    I maintain that middle school was the worst three years of my life, and though some of that had to do with the relationship between my parents, just as much of it had to do with my stature. Of course, there were people who loved and accepted me for who and what I was. I clung to those folks. The few individuals with whom I had a tremendously close bond were my world. Whether or not they knew it, they became my family, because when you spend almost forty hours a week at one place during your most formative and challenging years, you need a group of people there to help you get through it. But as loving as my friends were in middle school, it still wasn't enough to overcome the massive anger and emptiness that was storing itself inside my heart. I had no idea how to address or contain it, and as time went on and things became less and less bearable, it felt as if my anger slowly started encompassing me. There weren't many people I felt I could reach out to. My friends were nice, and they were good friends, but I couldn't tell them how I felt. They wouldn't understand. Neither would my sisters. Every day, when I stepped into Smith Middle School, it felt like it was me against the world. If the fight was a twelve-round bout, I would routinely get knocked out in the eleventh. No matter how much I didn't want people's words, whispers, or sly remarks to hurt me, they did. I did a fairly good job of hiding it. I would shrug things off and mostly act like I didn't hear anything. This was the point in my life when I really learned how to swear. Before then, I would interject curses here and there, as I believed some of my friends who cursed like sailors would interject. When you get people talking about you for most of every school day, you learn rather quickly how to give jabs and combo shots back, and most of the time, the sickest comebacks I could come up with involved multiple curse words. It was a small price I was willing to bear to get people off my case. As a result, I became a master at insulting people. At first, I rarely started arguments. After all, there was always someone willing and comfortable enough to remind me of my deficiencies. Some kid would crack some short joke or ask me how tall I was or how tall my parents were, and, just like that, the fight was on. The first few times I was rather timid, not because I was afraid of the confrontation, but because I just wasn't sure what to say. My family and I, particularly my cousins and siblings, had our fair share of clashes growing up, but we never really made fun of one another's natural characteristics. If I was out with my cousins and I happened to ask my aunt to buy me a noticeably fake pair of Air Jordans, well, that was fair game (and rightfully so). But growing up, I just never felt the need to poke jokes at someone because of something they couldn't control. I initially believed I could easily attribute this to my current state. Naturally, I thought, you're probably less likely to spend your time using your words to hurt someone else if you know how it feels to be on the receiving end of that. In retrospect, I've found that to be false during my start-up "fight back" days. For the longest time, I didn't even realize how short I was. It wasn't something that crossed my mind. Sure, other kids were taller and bigger than me, but in my estimation, it was no big deal. That was just the way we all were, and it didn't seem like something that would ever end up causing me so much pain and heartache.

What I've realized is that old adage your elementary and middle school teachers preach is incredibly true: the ones who are the loudest in the room and seem to feel the need to point out others' faults are the individuals who hurt the most; the holes within their hearts need the most affection, treatment, and attention. They're screaming and hollering for help, and they have been doing so for some time, but it seems as if no one is paying attention. They make it a point to highlight a source of your insecurities because, well, misery does indeed love company, and they salivate at the opportunity to attempt to make someone feel as despondent and lonely as they are. This is fact. On this point, I am not persuadable. I've lived it. In essence, this was my entire childhood.

    I became an expert at killing people's self-confidence by pointing out their imperfections—mainly because so many people had done it to me. I couldn't handle it. It wasn't something I was emotionally mature enough to handle, and I'd be damned if I'd have everyone pointing, looking, and stomping on me without some sort of retaliation. I became a master at hurting people's feelings. I was rude and arrogant—and unfortunately, I didn't know how else to be. I've often heard people refer to a so-called short-man complex. For a variety of reasons, I think that's baloney. Number one, you can sit down in a room with just about anyone for a few hours, ask them a slew of standard questions, and come eerily close to determining what ticks them off. That's called psychology. Even so, if short-man complex does exist, it doesn't fall on the shoulders of the individual who might seem frightening or angry. He probably doesn't want to be like that. At one point in life, he was patient, loving, kind, and sincere. He held doors open for ladies and relished the opportunity to smile at a person who seemed to be having a bad day. Who he is now, or who you perceive him to be based on two minutes of shallow interaction, is the product of people like you, who never fail to remind him of the many things in life outside of his control. In essence, *you* have a short-man complex, not him, because it's your insecurities that have robbed him of his patience and deprived others of his sincerity. This applies just as vividly to the girl who is overweight, the young lady who's taller than everyone, or the child's whose mother is white and father is black.

    The funny thing about insecurities is that they're a product of other people's inward emptiness. They grow and fester as a result of someone feeling the need to make sure he or she is not the only one with a bad self-image. Don't believe me? Have a child, one that is an ethnic minority, and write me a letter about the first time you had to talk to your child about race. For most people I know, that's a painful conversation to have with your five- or six-year-old, probably because for the longest time, the child just grew up seeing people for who they were. Skin color, height, weight, hair, and other superficial attributes didn't hold much relevance until someone, out of stupidity (whether learned or taught), decided to say that those things did matter. It's like people who conveniently get outraged when racial slurs are muttered, yet they freely join in conversations about people's height, weight, and even superficial things like hair or makeup. Newsflash: there really is no difference. At what point do people become comfortable poking fun at others, yet feel as if the same venom should never be spewed at them? Growing up, I was called both nigger and munchkin on multiple occasions, and I vividly remember the feelings of anger and resentment associated with being called munchkin far more than I do the feelings I had when called a nigger. In all actuality, being called a nigger or a monkey never really hurt me. Sure, I was astonished and appalled when those words came out of the lips of adversaries, but they didn't cause me any pain. Pain is the key here. Anger is an expectation of sorts, especially when it comes to racial issues. Virtually all of my friends were told to hit another person if that person happened to call them a nigger. That seems to be the norm for a number of insults we have expectations for. Some parents instruct their daughters to resort to violence if a boy calls them a bitch. The list goes on and on. At some point, it became acceptable to resort to violence because of racial- or gender-based insults, so why not other immutable characteristics? I have little respect for people who claim to be so ethnically diverse and culturally loving, yet their conversations and attitude don't reflect that positivity. If you think it is appropriate to remind me of my height in a condescending and hurtful way nearly every time you see me, take some time to understand how narcissistic it is to have an expectation that someone won't call you nigger, cracker, spic, or bitch. All of these slurs, and so many others, should be removed from our vernacular.

I don't know if I was sheltered during elementary school or if it was just the fact that I was about the same size as everyone else during those years, but the moment I stepped foot into Smith Middle School, my life changed forever, and not in a good way. To this day, I contend—and I expect to feel this way for the rest of my life—middle school was the worst three years of my life. I hated it. There were a few people there I loved and cherished, and still do to this day, but for the most part, those were three years I would love to erase from my psyche. They were the climax of my heartache in so many different areas of life, but mostly the things that made me feel so insecure.

Elementary school was easier because the pot was smaller. Fewer kids meant you had a smoother time getting to know other people. I've always been somewhat charismatic, so there weren't many people outside my grade level that I didn't know. Middle school brought a sudden and abrupt change to that. In an instant, I was thrown into a fire (otherwise known as a pod) with some eighty other students, most of whom I had never seen before in my life. The few friends I did have were scattered in other pods. I was by myself, alone in what seemed like a fiery furnace, and it was only the beginning.

A Crime to Remember

I'm not sure when it was, precisely. I just know it was during the first semester of my sixth-grade year. For some reason, we didn't call them semesters then, but quarters, and we got four different grades for the same course three years in a row. To this day, that concept still makes zero sense to me. I don't remember much about the circumstances surrounding the incident, at least the external ones. Things at home were fine. They weren't good, steady, or improving, but they were fine—maybe even becoming bearable. I'm not sure if I was just getting to a point in life where I had naturally accepted some things, but I was at least trying to come to grips with the fact that maybe my parents didn't love each other, my brother did have a disability, and, at least in my mind, there were many things I would just never be good enough to accomplish. As painful as things at home might have been, however, I was learning to navigate my way through my home life. It was the torture and hell I experienced at school that ripped my heart out of my chest each day.

It never failed. Every single day, either on the bus ride home or for a few short minutes after school, between finishing my snack and starting my homework, I would stare out of a window and dream of a happier place in life. I found myself wondering, at least for those first few months of middle school, what happened. Less than a year ago, school had been the place I went to in order to get away from home. At school, I forgot about the things I saw at home, the heartache associated with Russ, the fears that made my heart tremble and that I kept stored up inside. Life was life, and the realities of it were going to be present regardless, but when I was at school, well, those realities went on hiatus until 3:15 p.m. School was the one place I actually always felt like a kid. Going back and forth to classes and roaming the halls between math, art, music, and social studies was all I needed to block out pain. Don't get me wrong, it wasn't perfect, and there were still plenty of times when I failed to keep myself levelheaded and composed enough and my emotions poured out on the classroom carpet. However, for the most part, I was a well-trained soldier for about eight hours a day. Middle school changed all of that. The kids were cruel, and the school was bigger. The adjustment period was so much tougher than I had anticipated, and I didn't have many old friends I could lean on for help working through my issues. Even with all that, the most difficult part of the transition was that—you guessed it—the kids were just downright cruel, like disgustingly mean, bitter, and cruel for no apparent reason.

In late September, still attempting to settle into my new universe but not totally mentally drained or emotionally depressed yet, I decided to try out for the basketball team. In retrospect, making the team probably wasn't a very realistic expectation. Aside from my stature, that fact was that most of the guys trying out already had some connection with the coaches. Throughout elementary school, and even during the initial weeks of middle school, I would sit at the lunch table and eavesdrop on various conversations. And while a lot of the time, the topic of discussion was sex or sneakers, I also heard the acronym AAU quite a bit. I hadn't the slightest idea what it meant. After intruding on enough conversations and directing questions to people I thought would only marginally judge me, I found out that it had something to do with basketball, but I still didn't know how important it was. I also didn't know how much AAU meant in terms of popularity and fitting in during middle school as a young black male.

Growing up, at least until this point, basketball had been my thing. It was the game I loved and cherished the most. I had yet to be introduced to football, baseball, or any of the other sports I have passionately fallen in love with since. I was a one-woman man, and that woman's name was Spalding. For those first few years, it didn't matter that I was smaller than everyone, because few of the kids in my age group were giants anyway. Sure, there were classmates who were rounder than me, and almost everyone was taller than me, but the difference wasn't that substantial, and it didn't really hinder my ability to be competitive on the court.

Going from elementary to middle school changed all of that. I wish could explain why. I'm not sure who got together and decided that after fifth grade, you should go to an entirely different school and be confronted with an array of varying circumstances, but it seemed like *soooo* much changed during that one summer between Malcolm (my elementary school) and my arrival at Smith. Girls whose bodies had looked like mine in late April suddenly had curves and humps that I was unable to adequately describe without…well, yeah. *Everyone* cursed, though no one knew how, and it seemed like *everyone* had had a growth spurt—a massive growth spurt—over the summer, except for me. So it shouldn't have came as much of a shock when the sixth-grade boys' basketball team was announced without any mention of my name. On the way home from tryouts, my father did what any loving and caring father would do; he said all the right things. He reminded me that it's important to work hard and that there's always next year, and he couldn't help sharing the infamous line, "Michael Jordan was cut from his high school basketball team too." I respected him for it, and I'd like to believe I did a relatively good job of holding in my anger, but as so often happens when we internalize things without talking them through or letting those around us help, I reached a point where I could no longer function in my right mind. My emotions could no longer be suppressed, and I slowly began to lose the ability to control my outbursts, desires, and temper.

Looking back, I now know that I was simply not good enough to make the team. I don't think it had much to do with my height. Sure, if I had been bigger—with the same skill set—I undoubtedly would have made the team, but that's just life. It's a part of the cards we are dealt. There were other leagues I could have played in, such as rec ball, but the competition and esteem associated with playing at the local church gym just wasn't the same as putting that middle school jersey on, and everyone knew it. Rec ball wasn't as serious. They only practiced a few nights a week, and everyone had to play, and I have never been much of an "everyone wins" kind of guy. (But we'll talk more about that later.)

For me, it was never *really* about the basketball team. Back then, sports were a mechanism used to temporarily heal old wounds. (They still are, really.) No one cares that it's far from indefinite, because the longevity of it doesn't matter at kickoff on Sunday afternoon. What's paramount is the feeling that tingles through your bones and bloodstream when you hear the theme music and recognize that, for the next three hours, your greatest care in the world will be inevitably run off within a couple hours. And that's just *watching* games. Playing is a different story. It calms, soothes, and nourishes you in ways that nothing aside from the touch of a woman can. That's why I wanted to make the basketball team, because, at some point during those first few weeks of middle school, I came to the conclusion that making the team would somehow make me more comfortable with who I was, only because it would help me feel more like everyone else. Of course, that train of thinking seems relatively perverse, looking back, but when you're eleven years old and tired of feeling like you roam the halls of hell, you'll do virtually anything to relieve the strain and pressure on your heart. The boys' basketball team was supposed to do that for me; instead, it ended up being the final straw that catapulted me over the edge. I was denied the opportunity to have a band of brothers, or even to have an activity that I genuinely loved that would keep me away from the house five or six afternoons a week. Whenever some jerk would attempt to destroy my self-esteem or confidence with a short joke, I could chuckle in his face, curse him out, and wave my spot on the basketball team in his face. That's what making the team would have done for me, and though I do not believe it would have solved the majority of my emotional challenges, it may have made it easier to find an avenue to challenge the aggression that was building up inside of me.

It was almost the end of the day on a Friday. I wish I could recall the exact date or weather or any vivid and illustrative details that might better help you understand this story, but honestly, it just wasn't one of those special days, and this isn't a particularly special part of the story. If you asked me what led me to do it, I couldn't tell you. I mean, I *could*. In fact, you could read the last few pages and get a relatively good glimpse into my mind at the time. Even so, I am unable to explain why I felt that this day was the right day to do it, or even why I thought this was the right thing to do. I'm not sure how long I thought about it or if I even made a calculated decision to carry through. I had no idea what the outcome would be, and frankly, I didn't have any idea what to expect or what would come out of it. Over a decade later,

I still can't fully explain what was going on in my head. All I can really say is that I was hurt. I know, you're probably tired of hearing me say that, but pain is the emotion I am most comfortable with and have the experience with. At that time, in fact, it felt like the only feeling I would ever know again. I was tired of feeling like a second-class citizen because of things I couldn't control. Sure, my parents' issues at home didn't make school any easier to deal with, and yes, I was upset about not making the basketball team, but it was the constant jabs from everyone about something as superficial and meaningless as my stature that finally sent me over the wall.

As I left Mr. Calloway's science class, I grabbed a wrinkled sheet of paper from my backpack. There was something on the front of it—a school calendar, announcement, or old homework assignment. The ink on the front was inconsequential. The ink on the back contained the message I wanted to send.

WHO TO KILL

A Memoir: On Love and Life

Those three words were written in big, black, bold letters. I even took the time to trace over the words three or four times, just to be sure there was little debate as to what it said—and even more importantly, so it could be seen vividly from a distance. I put a few names on the list, mostly names of people who had made me feel inferior that day. In all honesty, if my goal was to put everyone who had made me feel inferior on that piece of paper, 98 percent of the people I had come into contact with at Smith Middle School qualified. I settled on placing names on there of people who had thought it appropriate to upset me most recently. It was the most convenient thing to do.

With the horrors of Columbine and September 11 freshly in the minds of everyone, I even wrote out, neatly and meticulously, "The best killing is yet to come."

Ask me now if I ever intended to take anyone's life, and I will, without hesitation, assure you that I didn't. I didn't have the heart to aim a weapon at anyone who stood as no physical threat to my safety or well-being. Physically, was I in a position where I would take someone's life? No. But I can't say the same about my mental and emotional state at the time.

A Memoir: On Love and Life

Most people who commit egregious acts of violence, especially mass shooters, give those closest to them ample warning signs and opportunities to provide an intervention. And while I do not believe mass shooters should be let off the hook for their evil deeds, I do believe that our public consciousness should have a hardy debate that is centered on mental health and prosperity rather than just on access to firearms. This is pointedly true for minority communities. The day I left that note on the floor of Mr. Calloway's classroom was not the first time I had hinted at taking anyone's life. What made that day different was that it was the first time I had threatened someone else's life. It seemed as if those closest to me just became numb to my suicidal tendencies or talk about death. I take responsibility for that. After all, the boy who cried wolf eventually ran out of legitimate and recognizable cries. For a while, my suicidal thoughts were just that, thoughts. Over time, I became enamored with death. The thought of death perked my interest so much more than anything that was taking place in life. I became fascinated with people who were also fascinated with death. In essence, I wanted to die— partly to see what it was like, but also because I didn't feel like being here anymore. At eleven, you start to understand the idea that death is permanent and that you're not coming back from it, but the legitimacy of your eternal nonexistence doesn't quite register. I'd spent a lot of time in church up to that point in my life and I believed God to be real, but in my mind, God didn't have much to do with what was going on in my life. Some people blame God when things don't go right, and their subsequent rebellion is somehow vindication, a sort of punishment to God for not making things all peaches and roses. I had those moments as I got older, and they became a staple of my life during my teenage years, but at this time, spirituality was nothing to me. I didn't blame God, but I also didn't cry out for His help, comfort, or attention. I was just tired of living and I was ready to taste the cup of nectar that didn't numb my lips and heart with pain. To me, the only way to accomplish that was by dying. I just didn't know how to make that happen.

  The summer before my sixth-grade year, I was staying at my grandmother's house in Maryland, and my cousin and oldest sister were also there. I remember spending a lot of the day staring out the window of the first-floor dining room. This one day was a beautiful one. Sure, it was a scorching ninety degrees or so, but I was content inside with the air conditioning and the Nintendo 64. I suppose that after a while, those amenities got boring, and flashbacks of domestic disputes and conversations about how some family members preferred not to be in the presence of Russ overtook my mind. In many ways, some in my own family made me feel eerily similar to how kids at Smith made me feel. Perhaps the summer before sixth grade was merely a precursor to what the fall of sixth grade would bring, and I happened to fail miserably at both challenges. If so, it wasn't the first time I failed, and it certainly won't be the last.

Whatever the case, that day I went upstairs to the room directly adjacent to the only bathroom in my grandmother's house. My cousin, Selena, was occupying the room at the time.

"Do we have any sharp knives around here?" I asked her in a calm voice. Since I had just made my way from downstairs, where the kitchen was located, I don't think she made much of my request, assuming that I was probably interested in a knife to cut a sandwich or a piece of fruit. As she hopped off the bed and started making her way downstairs, she kindly uttered a response. "What you need it for?" she asked in a calm, soothing voice.

"To kill myself with," I replied.

I shouldn't laugh, or chuckle, or even crack a smile, but looking back, I remember that my cousin's facial expression as soon as the *l* in *kill* rolled off my tongue was something for the ages. Selena went downstairs and grabbed the knife. My oldest sister, Yasmin, was lying in the bed in the bedroom to the left of Selena's room. Selena is a no-nonsense kind of gal. She's been through a lot herself, and catering to other people's emotions when they insist on doing stupid stuff hasn't ever quite been her style. She swiftly made her way back up the steps and grabbed me by the shoulder with her right hand. The knife was in her left hand. She opened the door to the room Yasmin was in and filled her in on the conversation we had just had. Selena, even after all that, was still willing to give me the knife. But she and Yasmin gave me a stirring pep talk, and I ridded myself of my suicidal thoughts for the time being.

I am sure that my parents, aunts, uncles, and cousins heard about this incident. I don't know how everyone reacted, and to be honest, their reactions didn't matter to me anyway. I cared nothing about what they thought of my stability, because it seemed like no one gave a crap about mine. Leading up to the letter I left on Mr. Calloway's floor, I had only thought about the prospect of death and what it might have been like. The incident that took place at my grandmother's house was the culmination of a yearlong saga that saw me warm up to the idea of never reaching puberty. In fact, as the first semester of sixth grade began to drag along, I became more and more fascinated by the thought of ending my own life.

When I first started exploring ways to kill myself, I didn't have many ideas besides hanging, shooting, or stabbing. As time progressed, I wanted to die, but I darn sure wasn't planning on inflicting *that* much personal pain on myself in order to do it. You can say I was a wuss…this may very well be true. I only knew of suicide from what I had seen on television or in movies or heard about from classmates or friends, and those were the only three ways anyone I ever knew of had taken their own lives. During that year, however, I started doing research, and it came to my attention that there were a number of silent and pain-free ways to go to sleep and not wake up. Perhaps, I had become too smart for my own good, but that intelligence didn't mean a thing. It was still ten years before my intelligence would matter, and I needed relief from this life of hate instantly.

That's what that letter in Mr. Calloway's class was supposed to provide, and in many ways, it did. I never even considered actually taking anyone's life, but as middle school became tougher and tougher to deal with, I warmed up to the idea of swallowing the white bottle of Tylenol my mother kept in her purse. It became my way out, and if this letter, in some shape, form, or fashion, didn't get me the assistance I needed, I didn't see myself walking around much longer.

As I walked away from my locker and gathered my belongings in my bag at the end of that Friday, Mr. Calloway strode up to me. He flashed the side of the paper with the calendar or announcement or assignment on it and briefly flashed the other side so as to leave little doubt about what it said.

"Do you recognize this?" he asked me.

"Yes," I said in a somber tone.

"Thanks; that's all I need to know," he responded.

He walked away. The bell rang. I went home. I'm sure I did something that weekend. I don't remember what it was. My parents probably had a fight that weekend, and I probably played video games well into the wee hours Friday night. Russ and I more than likely played basketball inside with one of those paper hoops I always liked to make. In other words, that weekend was as normal as most weekends, but a circus that I couldn't even fathom was calmly approaching.

Chapter 8

Love: **Help**

Some people will never understand what it's like to be suicidal, and that's actually a great thing. I hope most, if not all, of those closest to me never consider taking their own lives. I rejoice that thoughts of ending my own life are no longer a part of my daily meditation. Surely, my desire to forcefully bring on my own mortality was merely a part of that particular time of my life. There's a reason they don't let you even consider getting behind the wheel of a car until age fifteen, because, among other reasons, your brain just isn't fully developed. You haven't learned how to properly assess situations and adapt to unforeseen and unfortunate circumstances. Oddly enough, there are still people who find it facetious to remind me of my height on a daily basis, but it doesn't bother me much anymore. At this stage of life, I can unequivocally say that, unless it concerns improvement in my relationships (God, family, and friends), I don't have much of an interest in how people feel about or perceive me. I am so incredibly far from perfect, but I have learned who I should listen to or who just needs to call me "little man" to help boost their own sensitivity, hurt, and imperfections. This is a nice to place to be, but it did not happen overnight, and it surely did not come about without the sacrifice and compassion of so many around me.

The aftermath of Lettergate was something I didn't imagine. The potential consequences weighed on me the entire weekend. Nevertheless, I refrained from telling my parents. I didn't think I could trust them; I thought they would be more angry than caring. My childhood had been full of stunts and cries for attention, but that attention quickly transformed itself into a need for treatment. I would like to say that letter on the gray, dingy carpet of that classroom was *merely* meant to get a response and a few hugs, but that just wouldn't be the truth. I was so incredibly saddened, not only by the things around me but by the world I was living in. Truthfully, it started feeling like violence was the only means to a respectable end. In other words, being the outcast—the short guy who made good grades, wrote compelling short stories, and knew everything about basketball, that wasn't enough to feel like I belonged…anywhere. It may sound rather capricious looking at it through the lens of an early twentysomething, but this feeling is, literally, life and death during your early teenage years.

I went to school the following Monday like it was a regular day. I awoke, brushed my teeth, dressed in some sort of athletic or name-brand gear that was cool in 2001, and started out the door. The bus ride was as normal as bus rides generally were. My peers and I cracked a few jokes laced with a few coarse words that we still weren't exactly sure how to use, and we grudgingly got off the bus when it turned into the school parking lot roughly twenty minutes later. I waltzed down to homeroom, Mrs. Bach's class, and began to believe that my plight had ended Friday afternoon when Mr. Calloway had turned and strutted away from me in disgust. I ate breakfast at school that morning, and it turned out to be my favorite, those little cinnamon biscuits with the crusted white frosting on the top. I took my regular seat in Mrs. Bach's class and downed what felt like a one-ounce carton of orange juice after devouring the little bit of cinnamony goodness. Soon, my suspicions and expectations of normalcy began to change. Mrs. Bach was always a cheerful person; she *loved* teaching, and it showed. I gravitated to her, mostly because she was the only black teacher I had that year (and, consequently, my entire tenure at Smith Middle School). This morning, she didn't seem like her regular self. She didn't seem to be distraught by anything personal, but the vibe I felt when I first saw and spoke to her that morning was a mixture of concern and disappointment. She knew about the letter, and she knew the impending fallout; she just didn't want to tell me about it.

We recited the pledge of allegiance that morning, as we always did. We were all still in shock about September 11, so the pledge, at the time, took on a symbolic, foundational meaning for us. I recall mornings in high school when a countless number of students would exempt themselves out of the recital, some from utter defiance, others who were merely just too lazy to rise from their chairs. One would not dare to act that way in the wake of September 11. If you didn't pledge your life to the flag in those weeks and months following, you weren't an American. (So conventional thinking goes at least.) After reciting the pledge of allegiance and spending the usual six minutes being told to quiet down so we could listen to the morning announcements that no one really cared about, it was time to make our way from homeroom to first period. Today was one of those bittersweet kind of days. Our first-period class that day was connections, which, this morning, meant going to PE right after homeroom. I had a love/hate relationship with these A days. On one hand, school always got off to a roaring start, because you rode the bus with your friends, said a few curse words, ate breakfast, and then went straight to the gym. It was as if school didn't really start until 10:55 a.m., after we made the solemn walk back to our pod area and proceeded to grab our language arts or social studies books from our cramped lockers. On the other hand, since gym class was so early in the morning, the best part of the day was over before noon. Regardless, those A days were exciting. I didn't know what that day's gym activity would be, but it didn't matter; whatever it was, it was yet another opportunity to escape impending reality. There was always something about gym class during middle school, and though I cannot put my finger on the particulars, my plight for acceptance and perpetual battle with those who were insistent on reminding me of my physical deficiencies seemed to halt, temporarily, during gym. Maybe it was out of selfish ambition. After all, I was good at almost everything we were asked to do in gym class, and when it came time to pick teams or find someone athletic you could count on, I may not have been the first pick, but I was always far from the last. I guess I would say this was where my adoration for the game (any game) really began.

But as much as I loved gym and loved being able to start the week with the grand smell of a teenage boy locker room, that oasis was out of my grasp today. I grabbed my backpack and the plastic grocery bag that contained my change of clothes. For some reason, I was lagging behind the class today, and all but a few people had already made it out the door and headed to their connection class. Perhaps this was yet another example of intelligent design. Mrs. Bach placed her hand on my right shoulder as I simultaneously lifted my bags off the floor.

"You need to go see Mr. Lane, OK, baby?"

I already knew what it was. There was no ambiguity and absolutely no surprise. I didn't need to act stupid and wonder what it was about. I could have played ignorant, but that wouldn't have done any good. I realized, in that instant, as the word *baby* rolled off her tongue, that it was time to face the music. In that moment, it didn't matter what else took place. The consequences were something I would have to deal with, and quite frankly, I was prepared to do so. I had made the determination long before I'd dropped the note on the floor—I would embrace whatever came with this situation, mostly because I knew, unequivocally, that what followed could not possibly be worse than what I was already going through, the emptiness I felt inside every day. So as Mrs. Bach clutched my right shoulder and told me to make my way to Mr. Lane's office, I couldn't help but think, in some strange, twisted, and desperate way, that the mission had already been accomplished. The way she clutched my shoulder wasn't like Mr. Calloway; it wasn't callous or unforgiving or attempting to be intimidating. She touched me with compassion, and though her instructions had a sense of disappointment enveloped within them as well, I saw more love and authenticity there than any other emotion or characteristic. In that instant, I finally allowed myself to believe that maybe, just maybe, someone did care about me and my well-being, and they had a vague idea of how difficult it was to face the insults of hundreds of children each day. Lucky for me, Mrs. Bach's love was only the beginning of a magical story of reconciliation, coping, and redemption.

    The halls of Smith Middle School still reek to this day. They are festered with despondency and littered with bad memories. Though the words that were hurled at me throughout the years in those halls no longer dampen my emotions or self-confidence, I still haven't found the strength to ward off the disdain I have for simply being present in that school. Russ attended Smith a few years ago. I would take him to school fairly often and occasionally I would park the car and walk him inside to his classroom. With each walk, it got better. Every time I entered and subsequently left one of the four blue doors at the entrance, it became a little easier for my mind not to revert back to countless unwanted scenarios. It wasn't really about what had happened. That was in the past. By this time, I was a young adult and I was already more than comfortable with who I was and who I saw myself becoming. It's not like I couldn't pass the eighth-grade cafeteria without sobbing or stroll through the media center without becoming despondent. That was far from the case. Life just has a certain way of helping you identify certain things—

colors, music, melodies, tile, voices, clothes, television, and so on—with particular time periods of your life. It's why '90s R and B will always be my favorite genre of music and why *Mighty Morphin Power Rangers*, *Saved by the Bell*, and *Boy Meets World* will likely never be topped by any genius television executive. Sometimes, when I sit alone in a place where people aren't meant to be in solitude, like a classroom or a cafeteria, I'll think to myself how much I miss the '90s and what I would do to have them back. I said this aloud one time, foolishly, and had someone offer their two cents about it.

"Dude, how old are you?"

If they only knew.

That's the most irrelevant question in the book. It's not about whether I was five years old or twenty-five years old. Children aren't stupid. In fact, most of who we are is a product of our most vulnerable and transformative years. The times we may not necessarily remember enough to be able to articulate, but our senses, emotions, sights, and sounds remember the people, places, and things that shaped our worldview. When any song from Mariah Carey's *Daydream* is played, my spirit feels like it's 1995 all over again, and in 1995, I know no heartbreak, pain, or despair. Instead, I recall flashes of sing-alongs with my sisters and my mother when I hear the melody of "Always Be My Baby." When I watch basketball, I think of the fictional leagues I used to create in my mind, which my dad would often interrupt to ask me to run to the store and get a bite to eat. It matters nothing that I was "just" five years old, because I remember and cherish those times so much more than I will ever cherish sitting among hundreds of people and walking on stage to receive a bachelor's degree. Nostalgia has its pros and cons, but if you were to ask me how I feel when *I Will Always Love You* comes on, I am not sure any collection of words would do it justice. It soothes and heals my soul whenever needed. I can't merely attribute that to a few poetic words and a nice beat.

And so it remains, if TLC, Mariah Carey, and Whitney Houston take me to unimaginable places of warmth, Smith Middle School managed to do the complete opposite, and it did that for a while. After you enter into the building, a door stands about two feet ahead of you to your right. They call this the attendance office, but it functioned as the main office as well. I came here whenever I somehow managed to show up late for school (which wasn't *too* often). Once you step out the office, you continue a few feet, and then the hallway splits in three directions. Straight ahead is the entrance to the media center. If you turn left, you're headed to the gym, band room, and in-school suspension dungeon. Turn right, and you're off to the pods. Going left was much better. It was an escape from the dismay that surely waited to the right. But no matter where I was headed, the hallways were not all that inviting. I have always loathed fluorescent lighting, and the more I think about it, the more it served as a source of consternation throughout my tenure at Smith. As the lights beam down, the hallway splits again into three giant gaps: sixth grade on the left, seventh grade straight ahead, and eighth grade to the right. I suppose some solid PhD who graduated from Cornell undergrad and Harvard graduate school wrote an amazing dissertation on how middle-school-aged children should always be split up in an effort to provide the most effective education. I don't know. I do know that I never dared to walk down the seventh-grade hallway until the day I started seventh grade, and the same unwritten rule applied to eighth grade. Fear wasn't so much a factor. I had friends with siblings who would wander over to the different sections at their discretion. I just preferred not to. I had become too acquainted with being showered with insults from my peers that I knew visiting the domain of boys and girls who had already been through puberty would just make things much worse. My sister Ashleigh and I attended Smith together my sixth-grade year, and I made the fatal mistake of trotting over to the eighth-grade hallway to retrieve lunch money from her one September morning. To their credit, the eighth graders seemed to be a bit less callous in their negativity. Instead of making me feel like the scum of the earth, they masked it with grade-specific words and subliminal undertones that I was not quite ready to fully understand or use in conversation. I didn't feel like I was gum underneath someone's shoe. Instead, I left there feeling like I was a six-month-old wad of gum under a desk that was about to be cleaned as the school year came to an end. I suppose you could count that as progress.

So there I was, face-to-face with the halls that had made me feel so lifeless, so insecure, and so worthless in the three or four months I had been there. During my walk of shame to Mr. Lane's office, I encountered an entire class of sixth graders on their way to art class, a slew of seventh graders who had come late but were lucky enough to get breakfast from the cafeteria, and some eighth graders who just thought they would take the liberty of getting to class at their own pace. None of them mattered. The time between stepping out of Mrs. Bach's doorway and landing in Mr. Lane's blue-cushioned chair was approximately three minutes. And for those three minutes, there wasn't a word in the world anyone could utter to me. I was the king, and if you so much as hinted that you might try to challenge my rightful place in the world, I was willing to take any measure necessary to put you in your place. I knew punishment was inevitable. I had nothing to lose.

    I didn't even need to step foot into the office. The door was the kind of door you find in schools, with a window in it, and through the window I saw Mr. Lane's gray beard and his signature walkie-talkie hanging out of his back pocket. Mr. Lane had tons of better and more important things to do, so I doubt he was waiting for me. I think this was, for lack of a better phrase, my day, meaning timing and perspective aligned in ways I so desperately prayed they would for weeks before this fatal decision.

    We went through the office doors. Mr. Lane and I spoke for a few minutes. He had already phoned my parents. He started walking through the consequences of my actions, one of which was a five-day suspension. I gracefully accepted it, though it wasn't what I had expected. I had thought leaving the list on the floor was merely going to get me some kind of help. My mind was getting more and more violent, and I had experienced increasing violent flashes and rage in my dreams. At that point, I didn't really want to hurt anyone, but I felt my emotions slowly swaying in that direction. I expected everyone to be sympathetic to that, and to a certain extent they were, but protocol was protocol, and whenever a threat is made, rules must be followed.

The Counseling Couch

    Perhaps you might call me a prima donna who longed for attention. I suppose I can't argue much with you. I, however, see things a bit differently.

Whatever the reason for that encounter, it gave me an opportunity and provided me with the help I needed in order to learn how to sort through my anger in a positive way. I had seen and experienced some things that no child should ever be privy to.[10]

Before that time, I didn't know how to talk. I mean, of course I knew how to talk about sports and video games, but I had no ability to discuss how I was feeling. I used to believe that was simply a "guy thing." Society likes to say that young males are not good at expressing themselves, and I have found that to be somewhat true. However, young males do not struggle with expressing themselves *just* because they are males. Let's stop acting like the difficulty of articulating emotions is an inherent consequence of gender. Instead, we need to note that we don't do a good job of making young males feel like it is OK to share their emotions. As a result, for years leading up to and into adolescence, we (young males) begin to express what is often

---

[10] What you've been exposed to in this book is not even 10 percent of the many struggles I endured and experienced as a child. The other stories are either too personal or involve too many people who are dear to my heart, so I chose not to share them. Just know that there was a reason for the depths of my despair. Thank God for Jesus.

built up anger and frustration by resorting to varying levels of profanity and violence. That behavior doesn't make young males delinquent—it's actually a cry for help, and in some cases, as in mine, it was one final desperate attempt to survive.

I don't know how life would have turned out had I not left that note on the floor, but I am glad I did. That sheet of paper and those words scribbled on it got me the assistance I needed. Things kind of changed for me at home. My folks began genuinely asking me how I was feeling on a daily basis, and my sisters hugged me for longer intervals. A lot of the time, even when I was down or upset, that was enough to give me the spark that I needed. This is why I always try to smile at people or strike up a small conversation whenever possible. It is important to make sure that you do your best to make someone feel like he or she is the most important person in the world at that time, because you never know what your compliment, smile, or embrace may do for that person.

Of all the things that changed at home and at school after the incident, the best thing to happen to me was actually a person. Her name was Dr. Mary Chestnut. I was nervous about going to see her. I had always thought going to see a psychologist was something that was frowned upon. At school, some of the kids who would frequently go see the counselor were made fun of or talked about. This was one of the reasons why I always tried to avoid telling any of the teachers or administrators what was going on. I was already perceived as weak because of my size—there was no way I was going to add something else to be picked on about.

Dr. Chestnut wasn't quite Jesus, but aside from family members, coaches, and mentors, she had one of the greatest and most positive impacts on my life of anyone I came across. I suppose any number of psychologists could have done the same thing, but they shall forever remain nameless in my mind. Once a week for an hour, Dr. Chestnut had nothing else on her mind but me. It seemed like the entire world stopped spinning. I could forget about Russ and my parents and school. I could finally figure out why I was angry. I had a bunch of questions I wanted answered for myself and about myself, but I didn't quite know how to work through them. Before I stepped foot in her office, I was skeptical about what I would encounter, but one look into her eyes, coupled with a gentle handshake, put all of my anxiety at ease. Her office was cozy. She had big, huge leather seating and stuffed animals everywhere. It made you feel comfortable. As soon as you stepped foot from the carpet of the outside office to the oversized, fluffy rug in her personal office, you knew you were in an environment where you could say whatever you wanted and not have to worry about your trust issues being deepened. That was so incredibly important to me.

Counseling did a lot of things for me, but the most important thing it did was teach me how to walk myself through my own feelings. I learned that it is OK to be angry, to be frustrated and upset with the world, but there are mechanisms to help deal with that aggression that do not involve harming anyone, including myself. Dr. Chestnut helped make the future real to me. My parents had always tried to do that, but I had never really listened, mostly because they're my parents. At that age, you tune out just about everything they say. Everything that was happening when I was in sixth and seventh grade was all that mattered to me. It seemed like those years would never go by, and that life would be permanently defined by what I had to face during those days. Dr. Chestnut helped me see past that. I like to think of her as another example of someone believing in me before I believed in myself. She told me I was smart, that I would make something of myself, and that these troubles I was having were only temporary. My problem was that I kept exploring the possibility of a permanent solution to a bunch of temporary problems. Dr. Chestnut helped me see how valuable my life could be. Obviously, there were plenty of people before and after her who also contributed to that realization, but at the time, in that particular season, she helped drive that point home in a way that no one else really could.

Keep Your Head Up, Because You Are Beautifully Made

Rarely do I talk about my moments of despondency, mostly because I don't trust people to be respectful or sensitive to the topic, but these pages are sacred in that they serve as a testimony of the good works of good people and the sovereign Lord. The confidence and optimism I display now did not come without fault, weariness, or fear. Additionally, I don't want it to seem as if I suddenly have everything together. At this point in

A Memoir: On Love and Life

life, I have Jesus, and I have a greater understanding of Him than I have had in the past. I have family and great friends, and God has bestowed enough favor over my life to help me pursue the dreams most intimate to my heart. Even with all of that in tow, I still get down sometimes. In fact, there are days I wake up despondent for no reason. The weather may be nice, I may have spent the entire day before with a family member or lady friend, my sports teams all might have won, and payday could be right around the corner—essentially, everything could be going "right," and yet I may still feel sad for no apparent reason. The bad days seem to happen less and less as time goes by. Post high school, going into my college and early law school years, I had moments where I would sit in the corner of a room, not strong enough to take my own life, but not the least bit opposed to God choosing to end it for me at that particular moment. I don't know where these extreme highs and lows came from. Some of my heroes, most notably Abraham Lincoln, struggled mightily with melancholy and depression,[11] and an argument can be made that those

---

[11] Check out *Lincoln's Melancholy: How Depression Challenged a President and Fueled His Greatness* by Joshua Wolf Shenk.

struggles helped make him the great man that he was. I don't know if that is my story. I pray to God that it (a life of melancholy) isn't, but if it is a part of the plan, I pray that people come to know the goodness of Christ through my ups and downs.

Perhaps that is you. Maybe on certain days you wake up melancholy for no particular reason. Perhaps you have tried to or are thinking about trying to take your life, or it's tough for you to see the point of living. You could be the guy in your class who isn't as tall as everyone, or the girl who everyone makes fun of because of your weight. Perhaps your peers call you ugly, make fun of the scar on your face, or make crude jokes about you because your body isn't as developed. Maybe your parents can't afford to buy you a brand-new pair of jeans or sneakers, so you're relegated to the same outfit three or four times a week. Perhaps you feel like no one understands you, and no matter how hard you try, you can't locate anyone who can help you plug the deepest holes within your heart. Maybe you have lost everything you ever had, and there's no one around you to make you feel like life is still worth living. I want you to know there have been hundreds of times when I felt just like that, and in those moments, I ask God to comfort me. I ask Him to wrap His arms around me and help show me a passionate love that renews my faith in Him. It doesn't matter what anyone says to you; you have a purpose. You have been placed on this earth for a reason. Things may seem bleak now. You may not be able to see the light at the end of the tunnel, and you may not even be in the tunnel yet. Death may seem like the preferred option over life. Nothingness may come off as more attractive than a life of brokenheartedness and depression. Those things may seem true, but they are not true. In your own peculiar way, you are beautiful and artistic, and you have passion and purpose. As difficult as it may seem, cling to those things that appreciate and excite you the most, and don't let them go. Know that Jesus knows the depths of your pain and the fatigue of your heart, and he longs to repair you from the inside out. Don't give up the fight. Know that being different is OK, that moving to the beat of your customized drum is much more admirable than following a crowd with no idea where it is going. What seems important now will soon be of minimal value. Years later, you'll look back at these times and understand just how much you learned. You'll be able to appreciate all that God was able to teach you as result of you having nothing and no one else to lean on but Him. I am completely sure that there are millions of people out there who have been through much more than I have. I can't sit here and tell you that I understand exactly where you are coming from; however, I can say that I have had some pretty low moments. Regardless, I started to heal from much of my pain when I became confident, comfortable, and content in my own skin. Embrace your inner desires and fall in love with yourself. You are wonderfully, fearfully, and beautifully made, and don't let anyone tell you different.[12]

---

[12] That goes for you too, fellas.

Chapter 9

Love: For What the System *Can* Be

Most people assume that I have always wanted to be a lawyer, or that I had a pretty good hold on my plans for life at an early age—if only that were true. My dreams, the ambitions I hold onto ever so tightly now, were not always around. Just as I have worked to make my life at least a marginal success, I plowed just as hard on the front end to even to create a realistic vision for the future in my head.

I suppose we don't turn our noses up at people in their early twenties who don't know what they *really* want to do with their life, and I believe that to be fair. Somewhere along the way, we thought it made perfect sense to force teenagers into making life-altering decisions when they are not even old enough to order a Jack Daniels Honey Whiskey on the rocks. Expectations, well, they just seem to grow from there. You're supposed to move out of the house at eighteen and go to college, where, in the process of being subjected to professor bias and favoritism, you're shoved a bunch of stuff that's readily available on Wikipedia and then

A Memoir: On Love and Life

asked to regurgitate it in the form of a few bubbles two or three times within a four-month period. The professors give you a letter grade, and thus, employers and graduate school programs look to define you by those letters, by that two-digit number with a point in between. After you graduate, you find a job, and if you're lucky, you land a "career." By this time, you should have met someone special, exchanged previously written sequences of words designed to invoke maximum emotion and a false sense of indefinite security, and everyone celebrates because the ceremony is finally over and the chicken is still hot. You have some kids, buy a home or two, and work until you're retired, dead, or some weird but I believe certainly possible combination of the two. This is what you're "supposed" to do after high school. At least that's what everyone used to tell me.

So with that in mind, you'll forgive me for not having the slightest clue what I wanted out of life seven months before I walked across a stage and shook the hand of my high school principal. That time of my life, for so many unexplainable reasons, was entirely too surreal. During the first semester of my senior year of high school, my mother was working twelve-hour days, trying to keep the household afloat. I believe she might have been a little skeptical at first about leaving her sixteen-year-old son unsupervised so often, but she knew that at Osborne High School I had more support than a boy trying to learn what it meant to be a man could humbly ask for.

I owe so many of the people from that school so many pieces of my life. In the interest of not upsetting anyone, I will mostly refrain from names. My football coaches, specifically Coach Hayes, Coach Jones, Coach Floyd, and Coach Bullock, reinforced a lot of things my father drilled into my head growing up. Every day, I got a new lesson on what it meant to be a man: commitment, hard work, dedication, perseverance. They showed me all the intricate steps it took to conquer nature. Even so, football wasn't the lone place of solace and growth for me. After all, I wasn't six feet tall, and I knew football would end some day. But as I walked off the field on an unseasonably warm November Friday night, the finality of it hit me like a ton of bricks. (More on this in the next chapter.)

The next week, looking for something that would keep me in shape and give me something else to be a part of, I went out and practiced with our girls' basketball team. I never expected this to become a routine thing. A few of my buddies and I were hanging out around the gym one day, looking for something marginally mischievous to get into. Coach Lisa Williams, on her way to practice, asked us what we were doing.

"Nothing," we all responded in unison.

"Come play some ball for me," she told us.

We obliged.

I had been fond of Coach Williams for some time. My level of adoration for no-nonsense black women has always been extraordinarily high, and even from a distance, I could always tell she was all business. I loved that about her. When it came time to take government class my senior year, God was on my side—he placed me in her class. I had, of course, taken my fair share of history courses in previous years, but I had not been part of a class that was specific in its teachings of the political process and the Constitution. In so many ways, the class was illuminating; it was just what I needed at a time in life when I was exceedingly fragile and vulnerable but also full of optimism and joy.

A Memoir: On Love and Life

When I see something or someone I like, I go for it, and I knew I wanted Coach Williams as a mentor. She had briefly shared her background: graduated from the University of Memphis with a degree in political science. That was enough for me. She had gone to a big-time sports school and majored in one of the few things I actually had an interest in. Surprisingly enough, it was her class, along with the emergence of a skinny kid from Hawaii with a funny name, that began to inspire my interest in politics. After class one day, fairly early in the semester, I asked Coach Williams if I could speak to her. She graciously obliged. I went through the story as quickly as humanly possible: yes, I am going to college, but I haven't the slightest idea of what I want to major in, what I want out of life, or what my expectations should be. She chatted me up for a couple of minutes, and I soaked up everything like a sponge. In so many words, and with extreme brevity and confidence, she told me, "You should major in political science and think about going to law school later on, but you've got time to decide. That's just my opinion though. Do what makes you happy. I think you'll do good in [political science], though."

I haven't questioned her since.

That conversation took place early in October of 2007, and when I awoke on the morning of Friday, January 4, 2008, with an overload of news stories and pictures of this guy running for president who looked like me and actually had a realistic chance of winning the nomination, my path in life had been written in stone. I knew where I wanted to go, what I wanted to be, and how I wanted to do it. I owe that revelation to Coach Williams, and a confirmation of sorts to Barack Obama.

Now, just to be clear, this is not a ringing endorsement of President Obama or his policies. My political ideology has certainly evolved in the seven years since he stood in Grant Park on a blistering cold Chicago day and announced he was running for president. For me, particularly in 2008, it wasn't about his politics, or his proposals, or even his oratorical abilities. All of those things were reasons why I supported him so heavily—after all, I identified as a liberal in all regards—but that wasn't the reason for my adoration. If it were purely because of ideology, I should have just as passionately hitched my wagon to John Edwards or Hilary Clinton. There was something else going on at that time. His candidacy changed my life, and it changed the way we thought about politics, the way I thought about the system, about what it could and couldn't be—about what we should and should not expect from our leaders.

I remember standing in the kitchen as my mother, brother, and foster sisters slept. I'm not sure what it was about that evening, but everyone had decided to call it a night early. It was a little after nine, and I had the television on CNN. I watched as Obama gave a speech from Houston. He had packed Reliant Stadium, a football stadium mind you, with a capacity in excess of seventy thousand people, and he was telling us more about his vision for hope and change. His political ideology is irrelevant. Though his governance may not be timely, or as seasoned and ripe as people may wish, his candidacy, his inspiration, and the things he stood for—that timing was so indelibly perfect. At the time when football had been taken away from me and I was looking for something else to be a part of, something of value to hitch my heart, life, and soul to, his candidacy came along. It helped me believe in myself again, if only marginally. If a guy with Hussein as his middle name could come this far in a

Democratic primary, surely I could do something with my life that would impact the nation. It didn't matter what it was. When I heard those final words of each of his speeches, "Thank you, God bless you, and God bless the United States of America," I felt, I believed, I knew that there wasn't anything in the world short of making the NBA that I could not do. If a black man could become president, surely a "short" man could be a governor or senator, or maybe even become president himself one day. My parents and mentors, along with people like my football coaches and Coach Williams, had instilled in me a keen work ethic that wasn't going anywhere. At this point in life, I had recognized that my talents were undeniable, but they were somewhat limited and confined if I didn't work to expand those talents daily. Obama helped me believe that hard work could actually pay off one day and that my dreams were not designated to remain distant memories on my thirty-fifth birthday.

I wrote an op-ed about Obama my freshman year of college. The night after he won the presidency, a night during which I wept in public and hugged more strangers in my life than I had ever embraced before.

A Memoir: On Love and Life

We had a discussion in my public speaking class the next day. I'll never forget it. Never mind that, to this day, I still can't offer the most ringing endorsement of my public speaking professor. In my view, some people need public speaking classes, while others, well, it's just a gift. I'm not sure where it came from (practically speaking) but for some reason I've always felt at home, at extreme ease, and comfortable in front of a group of people or behind a podium. Words are so incredibly powerful, so when I get a chance to have people wait on my every word, I don't take it lightly. Needless to say, I didn't believe I needed to take some generic course about posture and pauses, but I was there. I didn't want to be there. What made things worse was that my professor wasn't the most embracing or compelling figure.

I wore my Obama T-shirt and hat that day, somewhat as celebratory thing, mostly as a victory torch of sorts to all the Republicans on campus. We struck up a conversation, and my professor blatantly and unabashedly said, regarding Obama's election, "It doesn't matter."

I was shocked and appalled.

A Memoir: On Love and Life

In retrospect, I can see where he was coming from and why he thought it was of little significance and importance, but he had obviously never spent much time with someone like me. Most people in that classroom had never trotted home at age ten crying because they just been called a nigger or a punch monkey by two guys whom they thought were their friends. Growing up, in every history or social studies class, I saw those posters with the faces of every president. In my spare time, I would study them, the posters and the men whose pictures graced it. When you spend twelve years looking at those posters, seeing no one who looks like you, it's tough to believe you can actually be on one of those posters one day, regardless of how many times your family members tell you that you can do and be anyone you want to.

In that op-ed, I responded as eloquently as I could at the time, instructing my professor, and anyone else who shared his sentiments, not to rain on my sunshine. That night was the culmination of nearly thirteen months—or really thirteen years of hope. This was how a seventeen-year-old boy felt. I can only imagine how those who had lived and grown up during the Civil Rights era were moved.

Politically, did it matter? You could make a resounding case that it did not. You could also argue that it has indeed mattered, just not in a good way, and in many regards, I would not argue with you. Long story short, Obama has made plenty of mistakes. If you're a Democrat, you probably believe he's made few. If you're a Republican, you believe he's made lots. I assume Independents fall somewhere in between. But love him, loathe him, or somewhere in the middle, his emergence from being the product of a mixed couple, a white woman from Kansas and a father of Kenyan descent, to the Oval Office, is utterly remarkable. He restored faith in the American dream to Americans who, at times, wondered if this country even still cared for them…if their dreams and needs even registered as important.

Before Obama, I had just wanted to be a lawyer. Now, I want to be a public servant. I owe my life to using politics, governance, and lawmaking as a tool to help make the lives of those around me better. Sure, politics has its grievances, but it also has its advantages. It's a means by which great, intellectual, and self-denying people *can* impact and change the hopes and futures of others. Most of our politicians may not reflect this viewpoint nowadays, but they can, because that's what politics can be. It can be a source of inspiration and strength, of moral aptitude and symbolic relevance. At any rate, it used to be. That it was in 2008. That's what it can be moving forward.

My Hope, My Change

I believe in the system, in America and its foundation, morals, documents, and standards, not because I see it with my own two eyes now, but because I can feel the hurt and pain of so many people across this nation and I can earnestly say we can do something about it. We can educate all of our children and feed all of the hungry. We can love and equally treat gays, lesbians, and transgender people without subscribing to their lifestyles. We can put roofs over the heads of the homeless and grow our economy and military without high taxation and the threat of war.

Of all these things, education is paramount to any degree of success; it's the means by which 99 percent of this country may achieve upward mobility. Thirty years ago, you could be done with school after the twelfth grade and get a good-paying job at a factory or warehouse. You could work there for three decades, supporting a family with that income. That isn't the case anymore. The greatest threat to our national security isn't foreign or domestic terrorists, it's our lackluster education system. What happens to the strength of the republic when an entire generation of kids, already born into socioeconomic disadvantage, is left behind because their quality of education is subpar because they live in an apartment complex rather than a $200,000 home? America is different, has been different, and will always be different, because there's the undeniable understanding that if you work hard, pray hard, and sacrifice, your efforts will be rewarded. Now, people are giving up on that dream. In Baltimore, some eleven blocks separate one of the most prestigious schools in the state of Maryland from one of the most underperforming schools in the entire country. How do we rectify this? What do we expect of these children as they move forward in life? If we walk into a classroom in an underperforming school on any given day, do we truly think those kids believe it when we tell them they can do and be anyone they want to? Sure, they need more role models and examples. There's a reason every black boy in America wants to play in the NBA—because we see LeBron James and Kevin Durant on television and in magazines more than we see Ben Carson or Tim Scott. But there also has to be an acknowledgment that the system, currently operated from a framework developed and instituted in the late nineteenth century, is no longer operable and optimal for educating our children. Our lawmakers and teacher's unions have to realize that there is a better way of measuring performance than having children bubble in circles twice a year with a number two pencil. We can't cut funding to the arts and humanities and limit recess and expect literary geniuses and etymologists to emerge—not when we stick them in one room for eight hours and send them to see the equivalent of a warden when they find it difficult to keep their mouths shut the entire day.

Sure, there is some level of personal responsibility attached to getting a good education, but a part of innovation and creativity is being able to motivate and inspire a group of people who don't know they need motivation. I owe where I am in life now to the grace of God; my parents; and the educators, coaches, and mentors who believed in me before I believed in myself. But what if I hadn't had those things? What if people hadn't taken me in as their own son, saw my oratorical and critical-thinking skills when the only thing I was concerned with was how I was going to buy a new video game or pair of shoes? The art of inspiration isn't solely the responsibility of the educator; in fact, it may not be the responsibility of the educator at all. Indeed, teachers are there to teach, but when parents aren't present to serve in their role for whatever reason, the community has to collectively step up to fill that void. It truly does take an entire village to raise a child. What we are doing to many of our children is cruel and can be easily classified as criminality. We are robbing them of a chance at success in life and masking it as an unintended consequence of sexualization of culture, slothfulness, and a pool of limited resources. I don't buy it. We have seemingly failed an entire generation of children, and some would have failed regardless of the efforts of the community. Pastors, counselors, firefighters, and everyone in between could have answered every call over the past two decades, and there are some who still would have fallen through the cracks. There are students who still would have chosen to skip school for the temporal allure of sex, drugs, or alcohol. But for every young man who would have ended up behind bars regardless of mentorship, and for every young woman who would have ended up on government assistance with three different baby fathers, even with a father figure, there's a boy or girl who was crying out for help; who wanted to be better; who wanted to change the world and accomplish his or her dreams but didn't know how or didn't have the means. There are so many people out here in our school systems and communities who are ensuring that the path to success they stepped through earlier in life is open to someone coming behind. To you, I say thank you. I salute you. Our communities, our states, our country, and our world need more of you. Here's to hoping this is a call to action. Yes, it starts in our homes, but when those homes don't present the most ideal circumstances for our children, we can help our educators by offering our assistance and selflessness. That means using disposable income to open recreational centers instead of buying a third or forth home that you will only visit twice a year. It means less reality television and video games and more time consoling children who are going through nightmarish situations under which we ourselves would have emotionally crumbled. It means visiting our local elementary schools and finding a young man to mentor. We can teach him how to hold the door open for young ladies and transform his mind so he dreams of being Mickey Arison instead of LeBron James. It means pouring our hearts into our young girls, hammering away at the fact that there is no glass ceiling if you work hard enough and that you can and will be the CEO of a Fortune 500 company that you start from your studio apartment. We have to start instilling these big, lofty aspirations into our children's heads at an early age. If your dream doesn't sound impossible, you're not dreaming hard enough.

  I visited a prison some time ago to sing Christmas carols and offer my testimony. It occurred to me that these young men and women, like myself, had dreams. They were five years old once, full of laughter and missing teeth, gazing into the stars on warm summer nights, and they thought about who and what they could become one day. I'm sure their present predicament isn't what they intended.

  Some of them, undoubtedly, earned their way there. There's no question about that. But how many are behind bars because we failed them? Because we let them down? Because somewhere along the way, we thought getting our degrees and putting our children into private school was enough to pay it forward? Our educators need a financial raise for all they do, but we also must raise them up emotionally, psychologically, and spiritually, and that means doing all we can outside the classroom to ensure that every time teachers step inside of it, there is a child there who is ready to learn, grow, and dream. That child must know that consequences await on the other side of the bell if he or she doesn't commit to *doing* and *being* better each and every day.

Politics: A Public Service

I once read an online post by a well-known pastor. In short, he argued that one of the many reasons he chose pastoring over all other professions is the impact it has on people. He said he would never want to be a politician because their impact is so incredibly limited; the groundwork that takes place on a daily basis is not conducive to actually changing lives.

I wholeheartedly disagree.

A Memoir: On Love and Life

For starters, we have an innate drum major instinct. We want to feel like the things we do, love, and cherish are most important, even more important than anyone else's. It makes us feel good about ourselves and our vocations. It helps us be inwardly narcissistic without someone calling us out on our pride. If you block out any context, surely pastoring is one of the few vocations that has such eternal significance. That said, I'm pretty sure this same pastor enjoys his tax exempt status and loves the fact that he can preach from his pulpit every week without worrying about threat of castration or lynching simply because he believes Jesus is the Son of God. Even more so, I think people are more inclined to make their way to a church or listen to a Bible study if they know where their next meal is coming from. Give a man a fish, and he'll eat for a day. Teach a man to fish, and you've equipped him with tools that will positively bear on his life until his dying day.

That's what politics can do.

If we're educating our children, growing our economy, providing jobs, and making sure people can afford to see a doctor when they get sick, we're doing a civic duty, and I don't believe those tasks to be any less important than delivering a sermon on a Sunday afternoon. Now, you've read up to this point, so by now you know that I firmly hold steadfast to the power of God and the eternality of the afterlife, but I believe politics can be used as a means to subtly disseminate a message of redemption to those who are lost.

Of course, there are many people who will come to know Christ and never know the name of their congressman or senator. Additionally, there are people who take politics too far, placing more faith in a man or woman than they do in their Creator. But, as with all things, there's a balancing to be declared. The saint who excludes himself from the political process is just as foolish as the one who puts his faith in it. Both are acting without reason and merit; each has reservations that need be discussed and diluted.

Flaws and All

If you want a perfect nation or a perfect world, you should die. That's the only way you're going to achieve that. In the interim, our focus ought to be how we can best make the place we have now better. People want a perfect America. She is not perfect. She never has been, nor will she ever be. She is clothed with great inequity and possesses a rather foul stench of her past transgressions: the removal of natives; the shackles of slavery; the blood of Jim Crow; the barrel of senseless murders; the weight of gender and sexual inequality. Her sins are many, just as ours are, and we could continue to harp on those things that speak not of love, or we can turn our focus to building this republic into a stronger, greater, more accepting land of freedom and opportunity.

As for me and my house, I choose to believe in America and to hold fast to her promise and her hope. I know she is not who she can be, but at this tender age, she is all our Father would have hoped for her to become. She is a bright, distant star in a faraway land as we wait for her rotation to come ever closer. She is beautiful, but she is not Photoshopped. She has a beauty mark above the right side of her lip, and her stomach isn't as flat as a Victoria's Secret model, but she loves us unconditionally, and she gives us a chance to aim for and reach our full potential. She is, for the most part, forgiving of our mistakes. She senselessly angers at times, and even, in our darkest days, makes us wonder if progress and evolution are really happening. But at the end, when the night has passed and dawn sits on that distant horizon, she reminds us that there's no one else like her. She helps us remember that with her, we can be anything we wish to be. We might move on to other women and even spend significant time away from her, in lands separated by vast seas and oceans, but it won't take much for us to long for the touch of her embrace, the scent of her skin, the liberation of her affection, and the intellectuality of her debate. She is ever growing, and if we want her to become better, we have a responsibility to help aid in that maturation.

God Bless America.

Chapter 10

Love: **For the Game**

Every year on Father's Day, I sit down and assess the landscape of the relationship between my father and me. I sit down for a half an hour or so and ponder, thinking about what I could have done better over the last twelve months. I contemplate the progress I feel he could stand to embrace. I weigh the many ways both of us have failed and mull the extent of our triumphs. I pick up the phone. The early years of life didn't require a phone call, as it was customarily a joyous occasion and an excuse to go out to a restaurant. Father's Day was a hassle during my adolescence, as circumstances and family dynamics changed. Now, as a young man, I call, and when I pick up the phone, I am neither resentful nor jubilant. I am merely indifferent. This is not a reflection of the relationship my dad and I have. It's just that holidays like Mother's Day and Father's Day tend to, in my estimation, do more hurt than good. Perhaps because the people I love have been bruised by their parents more than they have been nurtured. But I digress.

A Memoir: On Love and Life

With that as the backdrop of each Father's Day, it's only fitting that my next series of thoughts on those summer days are the memories we've compiled over the years. After all, there isn't much sense in holding onto pain in hopes of creating a grudge match. So when I get off the phone, I tend to sit for another fifteen minutes or so and allow my mind and heart to go to places my dad and I have been before. And, unequivocally, every time I drift into a paradise of a utopian father-son love affair, I end up in the crowd. Here there are about eighteen thousand people I've never seen before in my life; the smell of beer is as enticing as a woman's scent after bathing; there are long lines and overpriced popcorn and chicken fingers; and love is expressed with hugs and high fives among strangers in an area where a scoreboard tells the story of pain better than a Maya Angelou poem. Since birth, it seems, this, the fragrance, camaraderie, and sheer appreciation of an element of life I concede from early on I have no control over, is my secondary sanctuary.

The most enduring of these memories is the first Saturday in November back in 2008. I was almost done with my first semester of undergrad, and my dad, for whatever reason, had made his way down from Maryland. It's actually kind of funny, mostly because I don't remember a thing about the day. I can't recall whether I came home on Friday or Saturday or maybe my mother picked me up on Thursday after the SGA meeting. Or maybe my dad came to Carrollton, scooped me up, and then made the drive back out. None of the surrounding events ring a bell to me. Why? Because they don't matter.

However, I vividly remember that the Atlanta Hawks were playing the Philadelphia 76ers, and it was their home opener. We got to Philips Arena a little late, for reasons I can't divulge, but we made our way into the arena on our own time. The seats were amazing, just a few rows from the floor behind the basket. I love sitting there, mostly because you can see the play develop better than from any other location besides the press box. Philly had taken an early double-digit lead, and at that point, it seemed that all seventeen-thousand-plus of us in attendance were going to be relegated to doing a lot more talking and eating than we anticipated. It's the risk you take when you pay top dollar for sporting events. The Hawks, to their credit, managed to cut the lead down to single digits in the fourth and made it a compelling late finish. Then, the Hawks down by one in the closing seconds, Joe Johnson got the ball. Everyone in the arena who remotely cared about the game was on their feet, meaning kids were on their seats or on the shoulders of whatever male had brought them to the game—dad, uncle, big brother, grandfather. Joe ran his favorite isolation play. "Iso-Joe" as we became fond of calling him in Atlanta, did a few between-the-leg dribbles that were more designed to run out the clock than get the defender off balance, and he rose for a contested jump shot.

I don't think the ball even touched the net as it went in.

Instantly, thousands of people let out one of the most synchronized roars I've ever heard. I jumped up and pumped my fist in the air as soon as I saw the orange ball pierce the middle of the net. Then, just as I landed back on my two feet, there was my dad. He was filled with just as much excitement and adrenaline as me. His response was priceless, yet customary for my father: "Oh, shit!" he yelled.

Soon after, he shoved me. It was one of the best shoves of my life.

Athletes will understand this best. In life, there's the disrespectful, get off of me, something bad is about to go down shove, and then there's the "you did a really good job, that's great news" or "did you see that amazing thing/play" shove. This one was obviously the latter, and I enjoyed every bit of it.

I managed to keep my feet. My dad was clapping. I started clapping with him. The Sixers called a timeout, but it didn't matter, the game was essentially over. I high-fived about five people soon after, none of whom I knew before that evening, and none of whom I have ever spoken to since. We told one another good night and safe travels. I had learned two of their names throughout conversation during the game, but I can't tell you what they were. I'll probably never see those people again in life, and I am perfectly OK with that. But for two and a half hours on that one fall Saturday night, we were family, and having my dad there to share in that experience only added to my elation. That's sports. That's what matters.

Like Father, Like Son

A Memoir: On Love and Life

It's hard to explain my love affair with the game, partly because most people don't understand it. Some seem to think it's too radical, while those who genuinely understand where I am coming from are just as weird as I am. Consider this my attempt to explain it. If I fail, I assure you I won't lose any sleep.

I was plagued by insecurities growing up. My dad was an instrumental part of my life during my most formative years, and he always told me to believe in myself, trust my instincts, stick to my convictions, and live in the present while preparing for the future. He also never minced words. A list of his most famous quotes reads like this:

"People don't care about you. You got to be willing to go out there and get it."

"You black, you short, and you a man. That's three strikes against you already. You swing and miss one time and it's a wrap."

On what would happen if I were ever to go to jail: "I'll come get you one time. That's it. After that, you on your own. Take note."

"Hardhead make a soft ass."

A Memoir: On Love and Life

"You're going to be older a lot longer than you're going to be younger."

As a child, I didn't appreciate the wisdom being imparted in his words, mostly because I couldn't really understand what was being said. Now, absent a few choice words, I'm sure many of these lines will be staples of my vernacular as I raise my own son(s) in the future. But even though my dad was always careful to be brutally honest about the perils of the world while inspiring and encouraging me, it seemed the negativity in my life had a deep and louder voice. It didn't help that it felt like my parents were *always* fighting, but that's a different story. Life had made me angry, and though I think my dad did all he could to prepare me for that with the knowledge of what I would face on a daily basis, preparation cannot always serve as an adequate outlet. You can know a tornado is coming thirty minutes in advance, but if you don't have shelter close by, it's merely the beginning of solemn tune for the imminent.

Over time (no pun intended) sports became my outlet, a safe haven of sorts. In fact, sports probably taught me one of the biggest lessons of my life from an early age. I tried playing football once in elementary school. It was the fourth or fifth grade. Looking back on it, I can say with certainty that I have always been introverted. Though I didn't have a rough time making friends, I preferred to keep my circle of confidants limited, while also reserving the latitude to spend my weekends at home, in my room, and in my own domain. As a result, apart from a couple of people, I didn't do much outside of school with any of my classmates until high school. So, as elementary school started coming to an end, I thought it was time for me to find an outlet.

Although I had never played before, I told my parents I wanted to play football. In the years prior, I believe my mother had concerns about my physicality because of my size. At this point in life, though, it wasn't of much relevance. No one had hit puberty yet, so the size difference hadn't become a major issue. My folks signed me up to play for the Powder Springs Indians. I never thanked them enough for this. Powder Springs was the team on the other side of town. The Milford Warriors played right up the street, about a five-minute drive from our house, but I didn't want to play for them, because all of my friends played at Powder Springs. This is just one of the many subtle yet paramount sacrifices my parents made for me.

They paid the registration fee, the amount of which I am unaware. There were huge differences between playing for Powder Springs and Milford. For starters, Powder Springs was more organized, had a nicer field, and had more coaches to keep an eye on all the youngsters. More important than the softness of the field or the club's organization, though, at least for a nine-year-old kid, was that Powder Springs had nicer uniforms. They were absolutely gorgeous. The letters were stitched, and the fit was somewhat snug, like college teams' uniforms. But the most attractive part of being a part of the Indians instead of the Warriors was that your name was stitched on the back of the shirt. After a few weeks of practice, I got my brand-new jersey. On the back, in big, blue letters with gold-and-white trim, it read, CURTIS. It was one of the more surreal moments of my life thus far. After my parents went to bed that evening, I slipped on my jersey for a few minutes and just felt it. I rubbed my hands up and down the linen and wiggled my fingers on the stitching. It was so awe inspiring. In less than two weeks, I was about to play in a real football game.

A few days later, I quit.

If you ask me why I decided to hang it up, I couldn't give you a great, philosophical response explaining how I thought it about one night, wrote a poem, and came to the conclusion that my time could better be served in some other capacity. There was none of that, not in this decision at least. In quitting the Powder Springs Indians football team, I came face-to-face with my own laziness and my inability to be uncomfortable. I didn't learn this lesson immediately. At the time, I was more concerned about how my father would take it, since he had invested all of that time, money, and effort into an endeavor I had insisted I wanted to do. To my surprise, there was no pushback from him. He didn't constantly remind me how much money he and my mom had spent, or the other things he could have been doing during those sweltering August evenings when he hung out on the sidelines and watched me practice. His only words when I informed him of my decision were, "You know you can't change your mind, right?"

A Memoir: On Love and Life

I told him I understood. And that was that. I knew, without much further conversation, that playing football again wasn't an option for a while. I didn't want it to be. In fact, people would never guess it, but I had zero interest in football until I was seven years old. That year, in 1998, the Atlanta Falcons made a run to their lone Super Bowl appearance. With the team's innovative celebration dance, a near two-thousand-yard rusher, and a coach with health problems seeking to inspire an entire city, I became enamored with the game. Sure, I had *watched* some football games before, but I couldn't tell you anything about the rules. My heroes were Michael Jordan, Allen Iverson, and Gary Payton. John Elway and Brett Favre could have walked into my classroom on the first day of school and I wouldn't have had the slightest idea who they were.

  Even with my love for basketball firmly in place, I wanted to try something new. I wasn't ready for baseball yet; soccer, at the time anyway, was nothing short of boring; and Moms wasn't going to permit boxing. Football seemed like the next logical option. It ended up, temporarily, being a short-lived experience.

As She Stole My Heart

  As my middle school years went on, my love for football grew exponentially. I studied the game meticulously, recording hours of game footage in order to sit, watch, and analyze during the off-season. I started drawing up plays, watching videos of upcoming draft prospects for fun, and playing full, imaginary games with Russ in the living room using fake helmets made of paper. (We played outside in the spring and summer months—no helmets included.) Football, in many ways, became my first love. And in eighth grade, as I slowly attempted to come to grips with and accept who I was and what I liked, football became a huge part of my life. During the fall of eighth grade, I considered asking my parents if I could go out for football again, but I decided against it. At the time, considering everything I still needed to learn about myself (which, to this day, remains a lot), I made a smart, mature decision. I wasn't ready to play football, physically or mentally.

  My assessment of that determination changed some ten months later. The day I walked into Osborne High School wasn't quite as forgettable as the day I took my first steps at Smith, but the weight of uncertainty I felt was eerily similar. In the three years since the incident in Mr. Calloway's classroom, I had learned a host of different mechanisms to help me with my wandering beliefs and thoughts, and ironically enough, they were actually working. Regardless, during the first few days of high school, I couldn't help but think that I wanted to be a part of something.

Middle schoolers had been harsh, persistently reminding me of my imperfections, but I knew high school would be even worse if I allowed it to be. Lucky for me, I knew a lot of people at Osborne from relationships I had built in both elementary and middle school, but many of those relationships were merely surface level. At this point in my life, with the emptiness I felt about Russ, my parents bickering and fighting daily, and my oldest sister off to college, it was imperative I find something to grab hold of and not let go. Sadly, I can't remember the moment I decided to go out for the football team. I'm not sure it was an instantaneous epiphany. In fact, part of me believes that I made a decision to play high school football the day I quit the game in elementary school. I loved the game too much not to maximize the few playing years I had.

I joined the team rather late, as most of my friends had been working out and practicing all summer. While they were getting bigger, faster, and stronger, I was at home eating pizza and hamburgers and bathing in the air conditioning. (As if I needed to lose any time I could use putting on weight.) I walked into the double doors of the practice facility (you can call it the old gym) that stood right across from the cafeteria, and I didn't know what to expect. There are two sets of double doors. The first one is gray, and once you walk in, is a staircase immediately to your right that takes you up to the basketball court. There's no insulation in this part of this building; it's only about twelve feet wide, so everything, to your inappropriate sexual conversation to the rattle of your cleats, echoes in this vicinity. When I walked in, there was little activity. The cheerleaders practice in the old gym, so there were a few of them walking up the stairs wearing scant clothing. (This may or may not have been purposeful.) As I reached for the handle of the red double doors, the door on the right burst open, nearly knocking me in the face.

"What you doing here, little man?" Coach Hastings yelled.

"I'm here to play football, coach," I responded quite timidly.

Coach Hastings laughed. He didn't do it aloud or to the point that I would blatantly know how he felt about me going out for the team, but in his heart and mind, he laughed—I could see it on his face.

"All right. Walk in there, turn left, and knock on coach's office. Introduce yourself," he said.

I thought it was at least customary to ask a guy his name after he said he wanted to play for you, but I learned quickly this wasn't a place for the overly emotional. When your feelings get hurt on the field or in the locker or film room, you don't take it personally. It's meant to make you better. This is one of the thousands of lessons I learned while wearing the pads.

I got out to practice about an hour late that day. After I met a few of the coaches and got a locker, I was sent down to the equipment room. You can guess what happened there.

"I'm not sure we have a helmet…or shoulder pads that will fit you," whispered Don Bearman, the trainer and equipment manager for the team. He scanned the wall with shoulder pads affixed to it, and then he waltzed over to the shelf of helmets, intentionally looking for the smallest one. "See if these will do the trick," he said.

He handed me shoulder pads that were two sizes too big and a helmet that barely fit tightly around my temples. We jointly tightened up the chin strap and maneuvered the shoulder pads as much as humanly possible to help them squeeze my frail chest. "That'll do," Don said.

Some of the guys had seen me walk into the locker room. The reaction was fairly mixed. The ones who knew me seemed genuinely excited to see me, like they had gained another brother. The others, well, let's just say they thought I was more of a mascot than an actual football player. In all honesty, I can't say I blame them. Height is one thing, but height can easily be compensated for with superior strength, heart, and conditioning. I'm not sure I had either. The first week of football practice kicked my tail like nothing in life had ever before. For starters, I was enduring some of the longest days I had ever encountered, waking up at 7:00 a.m. for school and not getting home from practice until 7:00 p.m. There was no time for homework, not if it wasn't of extreme importance, because my body couldn't stand to do anything but bathe, sit up long enough to eat dinner, and get straight in the bed. I was a boy among men out there, and even though I know now that many of them took it easy on me my freshman year, I still couldn't hang with the crowd. I wasn't sure what I had gotten myself into, but one thing was for certain, this time, quitting was not an option.

It's Hard, but It's Fair

No, quitting wasn't an option. It couldn't be. I had quit the last time, and if I ended up giving up on this again, I knew I would give up easily on anything I ever remotely wanted in life going forward. My third day of practice, I was in the backfield on a passing play and ran an out route. The play was over, or so I thought. I was about three yards right of the right hash mark when someone, I still don't know who it was, took the liberty of doing their best Sean Taylor impersonation on me. I went tumbling to

A Memoir: On Love and Life

the ground, and, in an effort to break my fall, slammed my left wrist in front of my torso. I screamed in agonizing pain. My coaches and teammates asked me if I was all right. Saying that I was not OK didn't seem like a viable option.

That entire night, and into the next day, I wore a brace on my left wrist and thought, over and over and over again, that maybe football wasn't for me. As much as I loved the game, I began trying to think of other ways I could be a part of the team and eventually be around the game that I love. I could be a manager…oddly enough, that was it. There weren't actually many options—not many that would make me truly a part of a family anyway. Being a manager would be nice, but at Osborne, the job of manager was reserved for girls who had boyfriends on the team. Guys who wanted to be managers were seen as cowards—they weren't man enough to put on the pads, but they wanted to be around the game, so they handed out water bottles and cleaned jock straps. I'm not saying I agree with this assertion, because I do not, but at the time, with a high school frame of mind, that's just the way it was. As the clock turned to 3:25 p.m. and it was time to either walk toward the bus or go into the locker room, I realized that I didn't have much of a decision to make, and even if I did, it had already been made for me. I made a beeline for the trainer's room, got some ice, and secretly popped two ibuprofen pills. I kept my brace on and practiced marginally. Whenever I fell on my wrist, which seemed like an inordinate amount of times that day, I screamed bloody murder or winced in extreme pain. That was the price that had to be paid, and by any means necessary, I was willing to pay it. Just to make sure there wasn't any irreparable damage, Don took a look at it and noted that there were no torn ligaments. I did a few push-ups on it to confirm that it wasn't broken. This wrist discomfort and minor swelling was a mere test of my mental fortitude. It wasn't about my physical threshold for pain, it was more about me showing myself how much I wanted this—*if* I wanted this. I might have weighed eighty-eight pounds soaking wet that hot, Thursday afternoon, stepping up in the pocket and attempting to block linebackers that outweighed me by over one hundred pounds. My inability to make any of those blocks didn't matter. I knew I wasn't seeing the field my freshman year, and impressing the coaches with my skill level wasn't of paramount importance. To this day, that practice was the biggest test of endurance I've ever faced. For two hours, I needed to prove to myself that I wasn't a quitter; that I had what it took to play this game; and that my work ethic, commitment, heart, and dedication would eventually be enough to off set any physical discrepancies I had. It took a while, but as I walked off the field that day, helmet firmly in my right hand, left wrist throbbing and marginally swollen, head dripping with sweat as the heat and helmet began to irritate my already embarrassing acne, I knew that I belonged here. We passed the stadium where we played our home games after practice every day. I glanced over my left shoulder at the entrance of Cardinal Field. I knew there were hundreds of hot summer afternoons, weightlifting sessions, conditioning drills, and sacrifices to be made, but at that moment, all eighty-eight pounds of me knew I had found something to put my hope, life, and heart into. I could feel it in my own heart, but most importantly, I could see it in my teammates' eyes. Secretly, they didn't expect me to last either, and after I went down with a wrist injury, many of them were sure I would give up. In that one week, I had earned their respect, trust, brotherhood, and camaraderie. I had finally, by way of working my tail off as the most undersized person around, been invited to be a part of their family. I knew it would be some time before I felt the adrenaline flow and the nerves shoot up my veins under the lights of Friday night, but it didn't matter. I was going to get there, regardless of the price I had to pay, and I had found a family along the way.

Failure: That Which Teaches You How to Win

I will never be a part of any group or organization that teaches children that everyone is a winner. I do not care how old you are or what your background is. Everyone is *not* a winner. Sometimes you lose, and losing is precisely what can teach you how to win. Our children should learn this at a young age. Now, am I one of those people who attributes society's problems to a generation of near adults who grew up getting trophies just for participation? No. What I am saying is that sports is a phenomenal mechanism for discussing, embracing, and learning about the intricate and paramount nuances of life—namely, how to accept failure, learn from it, and vow to turn that failure into success.

A Memoir: On Love and Life

I know so many talented people. They all have different gifts and passions and have the ability to change the world in a variety of different ways. One young lady has a beautiful face and even more beautiful heart, voice, and soul. She loves God with all her heart, and she is not ashamed to let everyone know about it. She handles children with love and care and will surely be amazing at whatever she chooses to pursue. Another young lady I know is brilliant. She has been blessed with a passion and mind to study science. She's always wanted to be a doctor, and lo and behold, she has that opportunity in front of her. Another gentleman I know is an amazing musician. His ability to compose melodies and tell such eloquent stories in a few lines is one that very few can rival. Would you like to know what all three of these people have in common? They are scared. They are reluctant to step outside their comfort zone. They are afraid of failure.

I used to be that way, too. Lucky for me, one of the many lessons in life that sports taught me was not to be afraid of failure. You can't be. No successful person is where he or she is today simply because of hard work and a lot of planning. All successful people failed at one point, and odds are they became extremely good at failure. Failure became a taste in their mouth that they easily recognized, a scent that became a stench they vowed to get rid of. Of course, in the back of their minds, when they were starting up their charter schools, nonprofit corporations, tech companies, or private practices and businesses, they understood that they *could* fail, but the idea of completely failing at their endeavor never crossed their mind. Successful people don't go into ventures believing they are going to fail; otherwise, why pursue it? People do not believe they are going to fail at something they choose to invest a lot of time, money, or resources in. Do you pursue a beautiful young lady and take her to some of the finer restaurants in the city with an expectation that your courtship will end after three months? No. You have a plan. You are intentional about executing your plan and communicating it to the people around you who have proven themselves to be dedicated to the vision you have articulated.

 Because of sports, I am no longer afraid of failure. Honestly, a compilation of my entire high school football career would be ample proof of my embrace of failure as a means to success. Nonetheless, if I had to pick a specific encounter, it would be my senior season. It was the fourth game of the season, and our starting running back was out with a toe injury; thus, for the second straight game, I was inserted into the starting lineup. I had had an OK game the week before, and I earnestly felt that this would be the evening I finally had a chance to show everyone just good I was and how hard I had worked over the past three years to get to this moment. I knew I would be a focal point of the game, as I had gotten more reps in practice that week than I could have ever imagined. My body felt good. Aside from the usual nicks and bruises associated with the game, I did not have any nagging injuries. I spent a lot of time throughout the day away from football players. Instead, I kicked it with my lady friends and listened to more Eminem than one should probably listen to in a lifetime. I spent the entire day dreaming about the game. I was going over plays in my head nonstop. I would present myself with different scenarios and blocking schemes and force myself to make blitz adjustments and pickups on the fly. I had prepared my body for this game for three years. I had prepared my mind for this moment for an entire day. I was ready.

A Memoir: On Love and Life

It was the second possession of the game, our team's first offensive play. We were down 6–0. Coach called my number right away. "Base left, forty-two." This was a simple play. I was to line up behind the fullback and follow his block up the two hole.[13] The ball was snapped, I sprinted forward, and just as I reached to clamp down on the ball, it slipped out. Before I even got back to the line of scrimmage, the ball was on the ground, and the other team had recovered. At no point in my life had I felt so alone. *Never.* As you know from reading these pages, the majority of my earlier years had been defined by just how alone I felt. Still, to this day, I have never felt a greater sense of failure than I did at that moment. That jog to the sideline was the longest jog I have ever taken. In real life, it took me about four seconds to get from the right hash mark to the sideline. It felt like four hours. It felt like nearly everything I had worked for and all the preparation and sacrifice had been in vain. I had failed to do the most simple of tasks. This sense of failure hurt more than anything else ever had, mostly because I had let my teammates

---

[13] The two hole is the hole between the center and right guard. The center and right guard play on the offensive line. The offensive line is the group of big guys who protect the quarterback and block for the running back. If you still don't understand it, pick up *Football for Dummies.*

down in the process. Failing yourself is one thing. Failing others who you love and care for deeply is another. In a matter of seconds, I had managed to do both, and it was one of the worst feelings of my life.

Redemption

I stood on the sideline. Some of my teammates came over to pat me on the helmet and let me know everything was all right. Some avoided me. That's the nature of the game. Two plays passed, and instantly I started reminding myself of the many things the coaches had preached to us throughout the week. They were more interested in preparing us young men for life than they were in preparing us to play football. They were darn good at both tasks, but they knew that football had an expiration date and that for most of us, especially me, that expiration date was weeks away. Coach Hayes always talked about adversity and what it meant to be a man and overcome hard times. He would always present us with hypotheticals, offering most of these hypotheticals when we were in the eleventh hour of a workout, on the last suicide sprint, or when there was a look in our eyes that made it appear as if we wanted to walk out or quit. His hypotheticals always took place ten years down the road. Most of the time, in his hypotheticals, we were fathers and husbands. Coach Hayes could look into your eyes and discern what kind of man you were destined to become. In his mind, if you quit on the last set of squats or gave a halfhearted effort, you're going to quit on your wife when your marriage gets tough. If you're pulling up the rear end in sprints, you're going to sacrifice the joy of your children for your own pleasure. If you quit football now, you're going to quit on your family when you find out you lost your job and the mortgage is due in two weeks. That was Coach Hayes's mentality, and in all honesty, I still believe him to this day. I played all of these things in my head as I stood on the sideline shortly after putting the ball on the ground, and I forced myself to let it go. I knew I would never forget it, but I knew that I could not allow that moment of failure to define me. If anything, I was determined to turn it into a moment of redemption. Yes, the damage was done, and the consequences were real, but there was nothing else I could do about it. I had to face them head on and try to adjust and learn from them. I got back into the game and had one of the better rushing performances of my career: six rushes for forty-two yards. I hadn't reached that mark before this particular game, and I never reached it again. I had redeemed myself; still, we went on to lose the game. My fumble was not the sole reason for our loss, but it played a part in it, and I accepted that wholeheartedly. Nonetheless, I taught myself a valuable lesson that evening: failure is a part of life. Even when you work tremendously hard at something, there is a possibility of failure. Regardless, you still must make the effort to succeed, to go catch your dreams and make them a reality. If you never put your best foot forward toward accomplishing what you want out of life, you'll never know if it is possible. You will sit on your deathbed wondering how your life would have been different if you had taken a risk. You'll resent your children and their success because you will believe that *you* should have achieved what they have accomplished.

I am a diehard sports fan (just in case you hadn't figured that out by now). One of the reasons I love following sports, as well as playing them, is that it forces you to confront two of the most compelling parts of life: (1) your inability to control outcomes and circumstances, and (2) failure. As a fan of professional sports teams, I sometimes think that caring about sports as much I do is, for lack of a better word, silly. Even so, I continue to follow and cheer for my teams with extreme ferocity. At the end of each season, however, *every* team in *every* league is confronted with failure. Sometimes, failing is easier to accept than others. If your favorite NFL team wins only three games out of sixteen, it's much easier for you to accept your fate at the end of the season. However, if your favorite team wins eleven games and even wins a couple of playoff games, only to lose in the game before the Super Bowl by one point, that hurts. It stinks. It leaves you feeling melancholy for days. I think that's an important experience to embrace.

In life, there are only two things you can ever really control. The first is your work ethic, and the second is how you respond to situations and circumstances. That's it. It sounds good to say you have control over other things, but honestly, you do not. Sports taught me this. More importantly, sport has taught, and continues to teach me, how to grapple with some of life's biggest triumphs and disappointments.

As a Means for Change

Some people say that sports are to blame for many of the issues facing inner-city youth today. Specifically, young children are not aspiring to be educators, doctors, or politicians because they all believe they will be athletes and entertainers. I think such an argument misses the larger picture. Sure, many inner-city youth have a misguided belief that they will end up making millions of dollars playing a sport. Nonetheless, that misguided belief does not hinder our ability to turn their interest in sports into something that can help reform some our nation's most poverty-stricken communities. Of course, when I come in contact with children, I always tell them to aspire to be an Arthur Blank instead of Michael Vick. In the interim, let's use Vick and the game he plays to help motivate these children, provide safe havens for them to learn, and create incentives for academic success. I do not believe that sports can change and save lives;

rather, I *know* that sports can change and save lives, because they did for me.

I was blessed to grow up in suburbia. My family is not a wealthy one by any stretch of the imagination, but I never went to bed without need. Sure, there were always times of struggle: we had more than one night when a hot bath could only be accomplished by boiling the water, and there were times we used ramen noodles as spaghetti. Overall, however, my needs as a child were always met, along with many of my material wants. Though I lived a life that many would consider privileged, I still had my fair share of struggles and insecurities about what it meant to be a man, what it would take to succeed in life, and how to attack the world with the same anger and veracity as I attacked the weight room or the football field. Sports taught me valuable, lifelong lessons in all of those areas.

To this day, nearly every analogy I make is related to sports. My time playing football taught me how to overcome adversity, what it meant to never quit on the people in your life, and how much harder I would have to work than other people to make my dreams come true. If one sport, a few teammates, and a handful of coaches did that for me, I can only imagine the impact sports can have on other teens. Why not use sports more than we already are in cities like Baltimore, Chicago, and Oakland? Why not build more recreation centers and shelters where our children can come to work hard athletically, be uplifted spiritually, and be empowered educationally?

For all the time I spend talking about my days playing football, I should confess that my high school team wasn't actually very good. We didn't win many games. I won't tell you that our inability to win was for nothing and that it didn't matter if we won as long as we played the game hard, because that just isn't true. At every level, you play the game to win. Period. That's my viewpoint on sports, and that, no matter how old I get, will not change. However, in every sport, when sport is played the right way, there is only one winner. Sometimes, that winner is not you. As a matter of fact, most of the time, that winner is not you. Take the NCAA tournament for example. Arguably, it's the best three weeks of sports each year. Sixty-eight teams come together after a grueling regular season with one universal goal. But once that ball tips on Thursday afternoon shortly after noon, the dreams of those sixty-eight slowly dwindle. In increments, we go from sixty-eight to thirty-two to sixteen to eight to four. Only two teams play for a national championship. Think of it: of the sixty-eight teams who stood in joy three Sundays before—who clapped, cheered, and hugged one another while they rejoiced in the accomplishments they had compiled over the past five months—only one ends the season with real smiles on their faces. Only one team walks off the court believing they are champions. Only one team doesn't cry tears of sadness at the end of the tournament. In a lot of ways, that's the reason I love the tournament so much. These guys love the game. They love one another. They love their coaches, and many of them love their institutions. They play for the name on the front of the jersey, not the name on the back. Though there are people out there who are making millions of dollars off of their success, hard work, tears, and 4:30 a.m. workouts, none of that matters when there's a loose ball with fifty-five seconds to play and a slot in the Elite Eight on the line. When the horn blows, I like to see the pain and anguish on the faces of the young men and women whose season is now over. That realization comes with such a finality that it is incredibly tough to swallow at a moment's notice. Nonetheless, the pain I see on those men and women's faces reminds me of the pain I have overcome. Their faces remind you that, no matter how hard you work, how deep the level of your sacrifice, or how strong the deprivation of your desires, there are still times in life when we will lose. No matter what we put in, there are things in life that we will fail at. Failing doesn't make us failures. If anything, failing is a prelude to success. That's why I love the tournament. These men and women, no matter what direction life takes them in, will remember this moment for the rest of their lives. Forty years after they may have missed a shot that would have sent their team to the Final Four, they may still be unable to watch an Elite Eight game without reminiscing on the pain of *just* missing out on experiencing a shot at a national championship. But let's not underestimate the life lessons learned on the way to missing the shot: the discipline instilled in a young man as he wakes up for 5:00 a.m. workouts in the winter time and the deep love a sister has for her teammates that motivates her to wake up at midnight to run to the drug store and get her sick roommate some medication even though she faces practice at 6:00 a.m., an exam at 8:00 a.m., and another class at 10:30 a.m. before the bus departs for tomorrow's road game. Sports, and the family, camaraderie, and lessons of how to overcome adversity, failure, and losing, can and should play an intricate role in restoring life and hope back into the heart of every part of our American cities—not just the gentrified parts.

The problems of violence, oversexualization, lack of respect for authority, and inadequate educational opportunities must be attacked head on by us as a people, lest we sit back idly and watch our children and their potential go to waste. Rather than resorting to violence through fistfights and firearms, let's put football pads and boxing gloves on our young men. Instead of letting the media dictate how our young kings see young queens, let's teach them how to treat a woman, emphasizing to them that real men love one woman with respect and courage. Let's teach our children some discipline and authority by earning the right to chastise and put them in place. What does that mean? It means we have to be relational with our children, and sports can be an easy mechanism for providing trust and respect for authority.

The Lessons of Losing

I can accept failure; everyone fails at something. But I can't accept not trying.

Michael Jeffrey Jordan

You learn more about the character of a person in defeat than you do in victory. Anyone can play hard when the score is tied heading into the fourth quarter, but the guy or gal who is still throwing his or her body around late into the last period, when the team is down by three scores, that's the person I want on my team; in my locker room; on the practice field with me; and as a friend, confidant, family member, and spouse. I want a fighter, because I know a person who is going to fight is going to find a way to win, even if it takes a bunch of losing before we get to that point.

That's how I felt in high school. It's how I still feel now. I lost at so many things—with Russ and Katrina; with my parents and my height; with my fight for purity and companionship. I've taken a lot of Ls throughout life. Some of those losses are my own fault, and they have come as a direct result of my own mistakes. In other cases, I have been forced to help share in the consequences of the mistakes or incompetence of others. Heck, in some situations, the L hasn't been anyone's fault; instead, it's a simple result of the way time, space, matter, and God work. As Coach Jones used to say, "It is what it is."

That's exactly right. That's life. You can't control what it throws at you. You can prepare as best you can for every conceivable situation, but at the end of the day, life is more about how you react to the unexpected, not how you prepare for what you know is coming. Sports taught me that. When you're down 35–0 heading into the fourth quarter, you can pack your bags or you can keep fighting. When you've fumbled the football early in the game, you can soak your head in despair or you can commit to being better, ensuring that the same mistake won't happen again. It doesn't change in life.

One failed business venture doesn't mean you should give up on your dream of starting your own business. A C+ in public speaking doesn't mean you're not meant to be a fantastic orator. A denial letter from the school of your dreams doesn't mean that a law or medical degree isn't for you. These situations are what we in the sports world call adversity. Life is full of them, just as games are full of them. When adversity hits on the field or court, we settle down and make adjustments. When adversity hits in life, we settle down, consult the ones we love and trust, and make adjustments. It means that in pursuit of our second business venture, we vow not to make the same mistakes we did in the first one. It means that in our next communications class, we'll study harder and privately hone our speaking skills in our mirror on our own time. It means that, though nine schools didn't think you were good enough to make it at their institution, the one that did is now your dream school. You don't vow to succeed because the other nine wouldn't admit you; rather, you become committed to succeed because success is a part of who you are, and you will not allow losing to define you. In essence, you've had your fair share of losses, but those Ls, no matter how many, have taught you what it takes to win.

    We must use sports *more* to show our inner-city children this strength. Many of them feel like their lives have been nothing but a compilation of losses. Thus, they don't value life itself because no one has shown any interest in teaching them how to win. We have failed to equip them with the resources necessary to win at life. As a result, they resort to the destructive forces that teach them all of the wrong habits. They feel like they have lost at having a relationship with their father. They cringe because they look at the other side of town and feel like they will never be able to compete, so they accept a losing mentality that tells them they can never learn how to win and make something better of themselves. It is *our* responsibility to show our children what it takes to win. This doesn't mean that they will all relish in the effort. Some, even with access to the best of resources and the most caring mentors and educators, will choose a life of perpetual losing and will choose to never turn those losses into success and winning. They will choose to be defined by their past, inhibiting their future from becoming anything other than what they have seen in their broken homes or on street corners. That's all right, because at that point, that will have been their *choice*. If someone persists in failure because of his or her own wrongdoing and unwillingness to change, then that is a casualty I am willing to bear. That doesn't mean it comes without hurt, but it does mean it comes with a small sliver of peace that allows us to know that we tried, and though we may fail, the tears, pain, and anguish we feel as a result of that failure will serve as a source of motivation and pride for the next child who uses his failure to succeed. That has to be the goal. It has to be the spark that lights the children of our cities on fire. It has to be what we dedicate our lives to.

The greatest basketball player on earth sums this sentiment up perfectly: "I've missed more than nine thousand shots in my career. I've lost almost three hundred games. Twenty-six times, I've been trusted to take the game-winning shot and missed. I've failed over and over and over again in my life. And that is why I succeed."

Chapter 11

Love: For God

Greater love has no one this, that someone lay down his life for his friends. (John 15:13 NKJV)

When I started writing this book, it was supposed to be a secular explanation of all that life has thrown my way and how I used those experiences to make something out of my life—even in the short time I have walked this earth. I quickly realized that that wasn't possible. Hard as I may try, I recognized how completely unfeasible it was to tell my story without telling it in conjunction with my faith. I have made it through everything life has thrown at me precisely because of my spirituality, and no matter the demographics or dynamics of the crowd, that is a component of the message I simply cannot change.

How the Gospel Has Gripped Me

I love romance and sentimental gestures. In a lot of ways, I am a hopeful romantic. Life inevitably comes with its ups and downs, but in my eyes, there's always a hint of love sitting there waiting to pick you up when you hit in the ground. For some odd reason that I am unable to fully comprehend or articulate, I have always had a strange appreciation and longing for marriage. This isn't a newfound feeling for me. I remember at age fourteen, long before I had given any thought to Christ or my eternal security, thinking about how wonderful it was going to be when I got older to be married and have a family; to invite people into my home with my wife and watch sports and cook them meals; to have someone you wake up to every morning and share your hopes, dreams, and fears with.[14] For the longest time, I would wonder why I was thinking about that kind of stuff. While my peers were busy trying to lay with the next girl at any given opportunity, I felt like a relationship was always the best way to go.

In retrospect, I understand where this obsession came from. When I seriously started thinking about proposing to Trina, I would ask the individuals around me a lot of questions about marriage and its complexities. Those conversations merely reminded me of why I don't share my personal views on such

---

[14] Don't think I'm a weirdo. I was *not* thinking about actually getting married at fourteen, but I was thinking about how wonderful it would be when I was married in ten years or so. Just wanted to clarify that—if you've read this far, you've already passed 1,777 judgments on me anyway.

topics with many people. For example, when I would ask my pastor about anything related to marriage and the guys I hung around were in the vicinity, I would get this general vibe of negativity. In so many words, I would be questioned. I seemed to be the weird one because I was genuinely thinking about marriage, while all the others were entrapped in love triangles or sexual promiscuity. That, in more ways than one, built my wall up even further. Even without Trina in the picture, I still had a lot of questions about marriage.

When I became a Christian, I realized that it wasn't biblical to pursue or sleep with more than one woman. I came to the realization that the marriage bed is undefiled, but anything sexual outside of that covenant is outside the will of God. Thus, waking up to dozens of faces that were not my wife's was no longer an option. It's not like I got saved, read a few scriptures, and then the next day vowed to make a covenant with a woman. Instead, there was an acknowledgment that a huge part of my life, and what I considered a necessity, was sin. In essence, I felt like I needed the touch of whatever woman I could get on a particular night to keep me sane, calm, and comfortable. Then I found Jesus.

Before Christ, I found comfort in a lot of things, but one of the greatest sources of fulfillment for me was the romance of a woman. Now, such an experience could not be had without conviction overtaking the moment. Then I realized that this comfort I had become so emphatically connected with was now reserved for marriage, but I just didn't have much faith in the institution of marriage.

Forget about the worldly statistics of marriage and the fact that half of all marriages end in divorce. My issue with marriage was that I didn't have a single picture of it. I saw my parents' marriage, which had ended in divorce and wasn't exactly the *Mona Lisa* of marriage illustrations. When I say no one in my family is married, I mean *no one*. Even as far out on the family tree as my aunts, uncles, and cousins, no one comes to mind who has even come seriously close to walking down the aisle. As a young man, when you have no depiction of that, you can easily believe—by default—that monogamy is either a thing of the past or simply not for you. All this time, however, I believe God was just using this desire to bring me closer to him.

Marriage, in all its beauty, is a temporal illustration of God's eternal design. Marriage is what we humans have to help us illustrate the love that God has for us. The husband loves his wife as Christ loves the church, presenting her spotless because he constantly makes intercessions on her behalf. He is patient, kind, gentle, and protective. He kills his fleshly desires every day for the betterment of his bride and his family. Even before I knew Christ, I knew I wanted to love some woman like that one day. As I matured, God used this desire to show me that the most important covenant I would ever enter into had already been prepared for me.

When it comes to Jesus, the church is the bride. I am a part of that bride. As I edged closer and closer to the fullness of Christ, and as I have matured in my faith and my understanding of His sovereignty and goodness, I have acknowledged His pursuit of me for what it is: a never-ending story of love, fondness, infatuation, and grace. In spite of all of my inequities and the many ways in which I mistreat and am unfaithful against

Him, He continues to love me; to make intercessions for me; to not give up on me. He made the ultimate sacrifice with me on His mind. Even when I chose lust, adultery, and violence over Him, He never stopped pursuing or courting me. He wanted me to be a part of His family. In a flash, I understood that everything I was hoping to give some young lady, Jesus had already given me. Perhaps that's the easiest way to explain my obsession with romance, because the story of the cross is the greatest love story that will ever be told. As you may have inferred while reading other parts of this book, my desire for romance and sensuality has not dissipated. However, the source of that longing is something I now clearly understand. I had been waiting so long for someone to come along and give me her whole heart in a way that I wanted to give mine. Jesus has become that for me. I am content in who I am—my passions, ambitions, and pursuits—because I find my identity, solace, and purpose in Him. I am defined not by my grades, degrees, income bracket, or marital status; instead, I find understanding through study and application of the scriptures, and that wisdom is only available to me by way of Jesus.

The Sinfulness of Man, the Graciousness of God

I have been blessed to meet a number of people throughout various parts of the world. I don't volunteer that information as an opportunity to brag about my travels. Instead, I offer it as another attempt to increase in humility and decrease in arrogance. I am not perfect. I know this may be the eleventh time I have said this throughout these pages. I think it's imperative that I stress this fact to the highest degree possible.

You may have interacted with me in environments where Christ seems not to be welcomed. I may have been in a state of mind or circumstance, whether self-induced or coincidentally created by way of proximity, where my speech was laden with profanity and sexual innuendo. You may have witnessed me intoxicated, under the influence of alcohol. You may have heard me join in on gossip. You might have been privy to my coarse joking or been around me at a moment when I failed to cover up my feelings of pride. Again, I am not perfect. Nonetheless, I have spent this time trying to point you to someone who is.

Man and woman will always fail you in some way. We are human beings. We are imperfect creatures, no matter how much our skills in science, engineering, or infrastructures might suggest that we are not. If you look deep within this fallen race, you'll find people who genuinely love Jesus and have a heart for His work and calling. These same people will also make mistakes. That's a fact of life. There's a dichotomy present when one decides to truly follow Christ. On one hand, there's the acknowledgement that, as long as you possess this earthly body, you'll be imperfect—subject to the temptations of sin. And though you will be equipped with the tools of God (the Bible, prayer, fasting, etc.) to help combat them, there will be plenty of moments when you fail at this task. On the other hand, there's a part of you that sometimes still feels like it wants to be the master of your own fate. To put it another way, at my age, I always find that the back of my mind never fails to poke my curiosity. At such a young age, I sometimes feel compelled to spend a night on the town drinking. Often, I earnestly want to spend the night with the girl I have been dancing with at the bar. I find cursing someone out is much more fulfilling than simply walking away from the confrontation. All of those things are sin, and yet I have not always been the best person at avoiding those situations.

A Memoir: On Love and Life

I believe that anyone who says he or she is a follower of Christ ought to have a life that reflects that. People should know you're a Christian by more than your Facebook page and a bumper sticker on your car. Something about us should be different. That difference can be a variety of things depending on you, who God called you to be, and the particular person you are interacting with at that moment. Regardless, there are times when we fall way short of this mark. I fall short of it more often than I would like to admit. Nonetheless, no matter how hard I may have fallen into sin when around you; ignored my duties as Christian brother; or chosen the temporal, deadly pleasure of Satan over the promises of Christ, God still remains who he is.

You may be a person who has seen me act like an individual far from someone you would expect to be a minister. To you, I sincerely apologize. I have an obligation to be the best reflection of Christ to you that I can be. It's not about conversion, nor is it about me feeling holy or better about myself. I aim to be a great reflection of Christ to others because I know how much He has strengthened and transformed my life, and it would be abundantly selfish if my greatest desire were not to share that love. Even so, if you have been privy to any of my more sinful moments, it's also imperative that you understand that my shortcomings, sins, and failures are merely a reflection of my sinful nature as a man—they have no bearing on the power or awesomeness of God. Everything good that I have ever had or experienced, I owe to God. All the negative things that rear their ugly heads whenever they feel like surfacing, that's merely a product of my own sinfulness. No, I am not saying that God won't allow you to be tempted, but I am saying that God won't intentionally have you sin. He hates sin, yet I find myself entrenched in it more than I ever can let go.

There's grace for all of my sins. All of the shameful and ungodly things I have done over the years are covered by the blood of Jesus, thus allowing God to see me as righteous instead of as filth. The same notion applies to you. It doesn't matter what you have been through or what you have overcome—there's grace for that. If you've had multiple sexual partners before the age of sixteen, there's grace for that. If you wake up Sunday morning not wanting to go to church because you sinned by getting intoxicated the night before, there's grace for that. If you've had an abortion, there's grace for that. If you've ever sold drugs, there's grace for that. If you've seen so much pornography that you can't keep track of the videos you have already watched, there's grace for that. No matter where you come from or what you have been through, Jesus longs for your heart. That's usually a cliché we get at the end of altar calls, but I mean it as a genuine means of comfort. It doesn't matter what you have been privy to or experienced along the way. God wants to restore you and make your heart His. That's a how deep the Father's love runs for us.

Love One Another

Throughout this book, I have been emphatically (and unapologetically) bold and transparent as it concerns my faith. My story is not one that can be told absent the remarkable transformation rooted in Christianity. I firmly believe Jesus is the Son of God, and it is my prayer to see as many people come to that belief as possible before they leave this earth. In my mind, I am not sure what kind of person I would be if I did not cling to my faith with a fervency that led me to share the goodness of it with others. Faith is one of those things you don't treat as a hobby. Before I am a son, brother, or student or will be a husband, father, or public servant, I will always be a Christian. That is my number one calling. Nonetheless, I thought it imperative to take some time to remind us all that love is a choice.

Sure, we Christians have a responsibility to love all people, but it does not come at the expense of compromising who we are or unjustly subjecting ourselves to hatred or hurtful comments. This same train of thought also applies to many other people from various religious backgrounds. Most of the things that divide human beings are social constructs that humans have created that are infused with the power of prejudice over the centuries. Though I do not believe my faith to be a man-made construct, I am not oblivious to the impact that Christianity has played on imperialism, colonialism, and oppression. In the same way that I ask that you attribute all of my failures and shortcomings to my incompleteness and incompetence, I ask that the ills of slavery, religious oppression against people of other faiths, and all other travesties where people have attempted to use Christ to discriminate or enslave be acknowledged as an illustration of the imperfection of man—not the imperfection of God. As I touched on briefly in an earlier chapter, I believe there's room for civic disagreement on a variety of issues. One such issue of much debate right now is homosexuality. As a firm believer in equal protection of the law and the law of God as given to Moses and summed up by Jesus Christ, I encounter my own contradictions concerning this issue on daily basis. In sum, at this juncture, I am not sure how I feel about homosexuality, and I believe that to be OK. I do not think it is right to deny homosexuals the joy of a ceremony commemorating their union, but I find it difficult to call that marriage, only because I believe marriage to be a biblical term, and that biblical definition is between one man and one woman.

At this point in the book, you should understand that there are a variety of things I wrestle with intellectually, mentally, and emotionally on a daily basis. Some will label me a bigot. Others will call my comments discriminatory. Some will agree with me 100 percent. I am OK with whatever you decide. Ten years from now, we may look back at these pages as an illustration of just how delayed my thinking was. By contrast, this may very well be the beginning of a personal enlightenment for me, one that reconciles the two spectrums of the issue in a way that enables most intellectuals to at least be able to see the varying viewpoints encompassed in this conversation. To me, that's what it comes down to. I will never please everyone, and I am OK with that. Pleasing everyone isn't my aim. I do hope to be a person who sparks meaningful dialogue about important and difficult issues and conversations. My prayer is that this section, along with many of the other sections in this book, might serve as the starting point of such meaningful talks. And let this conversation not be limited to sexuality, broken homes, insecurities, or relationships.

    I have been blessed to be able to travel the world, all the while meeting and interacting with people from varying religious and socioeconomic backgrounds. I have friends who are Muslim, Buddhist, and agnostic, just to name a few. I have shared rooms for extended periods of time with people who are openly hostile to my faith. I've been called a nigger and a "porch monkey idiot," and I've been called an imbecile for believing Jesus is the Son of God. I cannot fit on these pages all the mean and hurtful things I have been called, nor can I adequately express the traumas that so many people of varying religions and ethnicities have experienced in a way that does their stories justice. What I can do, however, is tell you what I have learned from my many travels. As President John F. Kennedy pointedly stated in his commencement address to the graduating class of American University in 1963:

> *For in the final analysis, our most basic common link is that we all inhabit this small planet. We all breathe the same air. We all cherish our children's futures. And we are all mortal.*

In a similar vein, in the streets of Accra, Ghana; the mountains of Nova Friburgo, Brazil; the woods of Readfield, Maine; the concrete jungle of Shanghai, China; and the bars of East London, there are three universal languages that are embraced and understood no matter what place on the planet you may wake up: dance, laughter, and love.

So with that, let our love for one another be pure, genuine, and real. Let our lives be devoted to making the lives of others better. Let us live in a way that shows other people how special they are to us and that we care about their well-being and continued protection. A brother is still my brother, even if he goes to the mosque or synagogue instead of the church once a week. A sister is still my sister, even if she marries her girlfriend and doesn't believe in a higher power. The things we have in common are so much more than the ills that work to tear us apart. As we become a more global society, we have substantive issues to confront, but at the core of each endeavor of transformation, hope, and success, there is a continued commitment to a life of sacrifice and an existence that willfully works to love not only others, but yourself. Your sphere of influence, as well as your passions and purpose, will undoubtedly be different from mine. Regardless of where life takes you, be better today than you were yesterday, let someone who doesn't think he or she is special to you know that he or she is, and live and love like death is one sunset away. If you can do that, that means you're living a full life, every single day. And in the grand scheme of things, what more can you ask for?

Love and Life,

F. C.

A Memoir: On Love and Life

A Memoir: On Love and Life

Acknowledgments

With the exception of Dr. Chestnut and Coach Williams, *every* character in this book has been given a pseudonym. This page, however, is reserved for acknowledging the people who have provided nothing but love to me throughout my life. This list is not exhaustive, and I am bound to omit some worthy people. I ask your forgiveness in advance.

To God: Thanks for placing me on this earth for some (yet) unapparent reason.

To my father: Thanks for teaching me what it means to be a man.

To my mother(s): Thanks for loving me unconditionally.

To my sisters: Thanks for being my best friends in this life.

To my brother: Thanks for showing me how to love.

To my grandparents: Thanks for laying the foundation.

To my high school football coaches: Thanks for teaching me what it means to work hard everyday.

To Nia Duggins, Douglas Parvis, Hilary Tebeleff, and Jason Soni: Thanks for donating your hard earned money to this project.

To my pastors: Thanks for ushering my soul from death to life.

To First Lady: Thanks for inspiring me to write this book.

To CeAndra: Thanks for being a great mentor. I owe you more than this life will allow me to repay.

To you: Thank you. I love you.

About the Author

Frederick E. Curtis II is a third-year law student at the University of Maryland. Fred is interested in combining his love for children and sports with his commitment to public service. Fred lives in Baltimore with his *Netflix* account and Joe Flacco poster.

Fred is available for speaking engagements. To inquire about an appearance, please contact him at ministry.loveandlife@gmail.com.

www.ingramcontent.com/pod-product-compliance
Lightning Source LLC
Chambersburg PA
CBHW021141160426
43194CB00007B/650